A Practical Guide to Mindfulness-Based Compassionate Living

A Practical Guide to Mindfulness-Based Compassionate Living: Living with Heart is a step-by-step guide for those who wish to deepen their mindfulness skills with compassion for a healthier, happier life and more fulfilling relationships. It offers a clear structure as well as ample freedom to adjust to individual needs, starting with learning to be kind to yourself and then expanding this to learn how to be kind to others.

This guide consists of eight chapters that follow the eight sessions of the mindfulness-based compassionate living training programme. To enhance the learning experience, this book features accessible transcripts and downloadable audio exercises, as well as worksheets to explore experiences during exercises. It also includes suggestions for deepening practice at the end of each session.

A Practical Guide to Mindfulness-Based Compassionate Living explores the science of compassion in an easy-to-understand and comprehensive manner, one which will appeal to both trained professionals and clients, or anyone wishing to deepen their mindfulness practice with 'heartfulness'.

Erik van den Brink studied medicine in Amsterdam and trained to become a psychiatrist in the UK. He has extensive experience in meditation and specialised in mindfulness-based and compassion focussed approaches to mental health.

Frits Koster is a vipassana meditation teacher and certified mindfulness teacher and health care professional. He has taught mindfulness and compassion in health care settings for many years. He studied Buddhist psychology for six years as a monk in Southeast Asia.

Victoria Norton is a qualified MBSR and MBCL trainer with a professional background in teaching and communications management.

A practical yet rich guide in living with a wise heart.
Tara Brach PhD, meditation teacher, USA,
and author of *Radical Acceptance* and
True Refuge, tarabrach.com.

From the first page of this book it is clear that Erik and Frits have a burning desire to help people ease the pain in their hearts and minds with their MBCL course. Building on the wonderful work of their first book Mindfulness-Based Compassionate Living, *they have now produced a volume where accessibility is paramount, with the eight-week course clearly laid out to make it easy for the reader to follow and get the most out of their excellent, kind, heart-felt work. They have a gift for synthesising vitally important ideas into an easy-to-follow programme that anyone can access and benefit from. Highly recommended.*
Vidyamala Burch, co-founder of Breathworks, UK, author of *Living Well with Pain and Illness* (Piatkus, 2008) and co-author (with Danny Penman) of *Mindfulness for Health* (Piatkus, 2013).

Mindfulness-Based Compassionate Living *is spreading beautifully into the world and touching lives in transformative ways. This new book makes the work more accessible to everyday people. It offers us a personal training pathway for enabling compassion to emerge in our daily lives. The book is a gift to us all.*
Rebecca Crane PhD, director of Centre for Mindfulness Research and Practice, Bangor University, UK, author of *Mindfulness-Based Cognitive Therapy* (Routledge, 2009).

Erik and Frits have crafted a programme that carefully builds on the learning from mindfulness-based programmes such as MBSR and MBCT. From this foundation, they introduce compassion-based practices explicitly. There is a solid and compelling theoretical base to the programme, which Erik and Frits have thoughtfully adapted to make it particularly relevant for clinical settings. The practices and exercises offer the potential for a thorough exploration of compassion in one's life. In this practical guide, each week a menu of options is offered with the encouragement to explore and work with what is needed, possible and helpful at any one moment in time. I have a sense I will revisit its delights often.
Alison Evans, founder and co-director of the Mindfulness Network CiC, and core teacher at the Centre for Mindfulness Research and Practice with specialist interest in Mindfulness-based Supervision, Bangor University, UK.

This wonderful guidebook will benefit any reader interested in the healing power of mindful compassion. The authors have dedicated their lives to these teachings and have produced a clear and practical way to integrate the best of science with the insights of the contemplative traditions. I feel this eight-session approach is powerfully innovative and exactly what the world needs right now. I can't recommend this book highly enough.

Susan Gillis Chapman, Vancouver, Canada, Faculty for Karuna Training, Acharya, Buddhist teacher and author of *The Five Keys To Mindful Communication* (Shambhala, 2012).

This pragmatic and user-friendly workbook brings forth a powerful integration of compassion practices for people who have some mindfulness experience 'under their belts' already. Underpinned by evolutionary understanding of why human beings are so driven to bring hurt to ourselves and others, it provides a supported pathway for people to meet and transform distress, and connect with their capacity to feel and express more kindness and compassion moment by moment in their lives. May many be touched by it!

Timothea Goddard, Sydney, Australia, Founding Director of Openground Mindfulness Programs and Mindfulness Training Institute – Australia and New Zealand.

This is a thoroughly friendly book, in which the authors show great care and respect for their readers, both service users and professionals. The work is very down-to earth and accessible, including vivid and engaging examples, poems and stories to encourage the reader on this life-changing journey. The Mindfulness-Based Compassionate Living course detailed here is closely based on mindfulness with the same experiential method of learning, and deepens that knowledge into heartfulness. I very much enjoyed this book and am sure that many will benefit from it by learning how to make the comfort of compassion for themselves and others an essential, fundamental part of their lives.

Judith Soulsby, senior teacher and trainer with the Centre for Mindfulness Research & Practice, Bangor University, UK, and certified teacher and teacher trainer with the Center for Mindful Self-Compassion.

A Practical Guide to Mindfulness-Based Compassionate Living

■ Living with Heart

Erik van den Brink and Frits Koster with Victoria Norton

Foreword by Prof. Mark Williams

Routledge
Taylor & Francis Group

LONDON AND NEW YORK

First published 2018
by Routledge
2 Park Square, Milton Park, Abingdon, Oxon OX14 4RN

and by Routledge
711 Third Avenue, New York, NY 10017

Routledge is an imprint of the Taylor & Francis Group, an informa business

British Library Cataloguing-in-Publication Data
A catalogue record for this book is available from the British Library

Library of Congress Cataloging-in-Publication Data
A catalog record for this book has been requested

ISBN: 978-1-138-22892-4 (hbk)
ISBN: 978-1-138-22893-1 (pbk)
ISBN: 978-1-315-26849-1 (ebk)

Typeset in Stone Serif
by Apex CoVantage, LLC

eResources available: www.routledge.com/9781138228931

The rainbow of compassion arises when the sunrays of kindness touch upon the tears of suffering.

—Tibetan saying

Contents

Foreword by Mark Williams

I suppose he must have been about three years old. He was on the bus with his mother, sitting in a seat a little in front of me as the rush-hour traffic edged slowly up Headington Hill and out of Oxford city. He was by turns restless and still – one moment entangling himself in her shopping, then on her knee looking out of the window. I found myself reflecting that this little child would probably see the year 2100. He'll be over 80 years old. By then, he will, no doubt, have known something of love and of loss, and have discovered his share of strength and of fragility. And through it all, especially at those moments of vulnerability, he will not only need people around him who are loving and compassionate, he will need to have learned to be gentle with himself. It was impossible to look at that little child and not to wish him well for his life.

Erik van den Brink, Frits Koster and Victoria Norton start by encouraging each of us to reflect on our lives in this way:

> Even if you were lucky enough to have a fair start and were raised in a warm and loving family, in relatively peaceful and prosperous circumstances, you will sooner or later encounter difficulties, smaller or bigger traumas, frustrations and losses. Even if you feel fine at the moment, you know you are going to grow old and die and eventually lose all that is dear to you. The world is impermanent, largely uncontrollable and practically unpredictable.
>
> ... This is exactly where compassion begins. When we realise suffering is inevitable because we live in an imperfect body, in an imperfect world, with many others who are just as imperfect as we are, compassion is not a luxury but a basic need.

'Not a luxury, but a basic need.'

Here is the foundational statement of their wonderful book. Compassion is a basic need. Yet, as they point out, it is something of a challenge to make compassion a guiding value in our lives. Why is this?

First, compassion is challenging because it seems so obvious and important, we imagine we *already* know how to be compassionate. After all, haven't we been told by parents and grandparents, by priests and school teachers and by – well, by any newspaper or magazine that cares to tell us what's good for us – that it is important to be kind, loving and compassionate? Isn't it part of the commandments and precepts of religion and fundamental to a humanist perennial philosophy?

But what is most obvious and important isn't always simple or straightforward. Compassion may be demanding, but it cannot be demanded. It's not that compassion has been over-sold, but that it has been over-told. *Telling* people to love may change behaviour temporarily, but it has a short half-life. We need a different approach, and this book takes us by the hand and leads us gently away from the mere *idea* of compassion towards the *experience* of compassion.

Second, compassion is challenging because, while most of us are aware of the need to be loving to *others*, few of us are ever shown how to be compassionate to the being we call 'me'. Why ever not? Because we have become locked into the idea that to love *this* body and mind is just self-serving egotism, unworthy, undeserved, or only for the weak. So we drive ourselves harder and harder, striving until exhausted. We do this despite our loved-ones' concern and our best friends' advice. Caught up in constant 'driven-doing', we don't take the time to nourish ourselves. So, like a metal spring that is pulled out of shape, losing its 'springiness', we too get pulled out of shape, losing our ability to see clearly and respond sensitively to the needs of the moment.

'Retaining our shape' in the midst of pressures that would distort who we are takes practice. What is there to practice? The authors show that there are practical ways to learn compassion that have been honed over hundreds of years. They draw on recent ground-breaking work by Paul Gilbert, Barbara Fredrickson, Kristin Neff and Christopher Germer to inform the programme they offer. These practices have been shown by the modern methods of clinical trials, laboratory experiment and neuroscience to be effective and life-changing.

Their book guides us through the landscape of our daily lives, offering new perspectives. It invites us to read, then reflect, then practice. It helps us explore, step by step, how to reverse the habits of a lifetime, and cultivate compassion that goes both ways, outwards to others, and inwards to refresh and renew the deepest part of ourselves.

In deep gratitude to Erik, Frits and Victoria for their work, I warmly commend this book to you.

Mark Williams
Emeritus Professor of Clinical Psychology
University of Oxford

Acknowledgements

Many people have contributed in one way or another to the creation of this book. A book like this is written in the span of a year, but it is the result of our life's journeys. We feel deep gratitude towards all teachers, mentors and companions we met on the way, in our personal and professional lives. Special thanks to...

People who have inspired us

In the field of mindfulness we express our deep appreciation of the work of Jon Kabat-Zinn, as the founder of MBSR, and Zindel Segal, Mark Williams and John Teasdale, as the founders of MBCT. Thanks to their powerful programmes we could pioneer mindfulness-based interventions in the mental health setting in the Netherlands. Besides building on their work, MBCL integrates insights from Compassion Focused Therapy (CFT), Acceptance and Commitment Therapy (ACT) and Positive Psychology. The compassion-focus in MBCL was greatly supported by the work of Paul Gilbert, the founder of CFT, and by Tara Brach, Christopher Germer, Kristin Neff and Sharon Salzberg, who all inspired themes and exercises of the MBCL programme. We were further nourished by the work of Barbara Fredrickson, Rick Hanson, Thupten Jinpa, Matthieu Ricard, Martin Seligman, Daniel Siegel, and many others. We are very grateful for their generosity in sharing their liberating insights with the world.

People we have been working with

We especially thank all the participants, patients and clients, professionals and colleagues, near and far, who shared in the evolving process of MBCL, by spending their time and energy following our courses and teaching seminars. We feel immensely grateful for their courage to be vulnerable and to openly share their struggles with life, and for giving us valuable feedback and suggestions for further improvement of the programme. We thank the mindfulness teachers who joined us in teaching MBCL for their valuable peer supervision, and the researchers for their commitment to study the programme. It would be impossible to mention all their names but we wish to express our heartfelt thanks to everyone involved.

People who have been facilitating us

We deeply appreciate the support from Rebecca Crane and the Centre for Mindfulness Research and Practice at Bangor, Alison Evans and the Mindfulness Network CiC, Hannah Gilbert and Compassionate Wellbeing, and Linda Lehrhaupt and the Institute for Mindfulness-Based Approaches, enabling us to teach MBCL in the English-speaking world. Many thanks to Eluned Gold, Robert Marx, Bridgette O'Neill and Judith Soulsby for facilitating the introduction of MBCL in the UK, to Sister Stan and Maureen Treanor for their support in Ireland, and to Timothea Goddard for introducing MBCL in Australia. We feel immensely grateful to Joanne Forshaw, Charlotte Taylor, Helen Evans and everyone else at Routledge/ Taylor & Francis who supported us in making this publication possible. We feel deep gratitude to Mark Williams for his heart-warming foreword. Many thanks also to Fop Smit for the illustrations.

Our loved ones

Last but not least, we would like to thank the dear ones in our personal lives who offered us a safe place while working on the book. The gratitude we feel towards our compassionate companions and beloved partners for their patience and support during the writing process, is beyond words.

Erik, Frits and Victoria

Spring 2018

Introduction:
a warm welcome

Let your heart guide you.
It whispers softly, so listen closely.

—Anonymous

What made you pick up this book? Maybe it was recommended to you by someone. Maybe you thought you could use more self-compassion or should be more compassionate towards others, or you wish to find more balance between caring for others and yourself. Maybe you sensed the need to find a healthier way to relate to life's difficulties or you simply want to lead a more meaningful life. These are all good reasons for carrying on reading. Maybe the practice of mindfulness has long been familiar to you; maybe you have only recently made acquaintance with it. In case you need to refresh your memory, here is a short introduction.

The gift of mindfulness

Mindfulness is something far easier to demonstrate than explain. This is why very often one of the first exercises of a mindfulness course is to examine and eat a raisin. Your teacher might ask you to imagine you have just landed on the earth from a faraway planet in another galaxy and you have never seen one of these funny wrinkly little brown things before. So, you let go of all your ideas about raisins. Looking at, feeling, smelling, tasting this object magically become completely fresh experiences. You might even be surprised to discover that although you thought you detested dried grapes, this one tastes delicious or at least perhaps not as bad as you expected. For a moment you let go of your biases and get into contact with your direct experience. This is just what mindfulness is: observing our actual experience as it enfolds moment by moment, with kind curiosity and an open, non-judgmental mind.

Mindfulness can be considered as a great friend in life, as it opens our awareness of life as it is. If we open our senses we become more intensely aware of natural beauty, the sound of birds, the aroma of freshly brewed coffee, the kind gesture of a fellow commuter. Fair enough, you might say, if life offers pleasant moments, but what if life gives you pain and misery? What about when you miss the bus, the dishwasher breaks down and floods the kitchen or the dog is sick on the carpet? Or even worse, when you lose your job, your relationship breaks up, or you get a cancer diagnosis? Why on earth would you want to be more aware of those moments?

Well, when we can see what goes on at such moments and understand ourselves better, it enables us to deal better with these difficulties. Life may itself be hard enough already, but our automatic reactions to what happens often increase our suffering and this is exactly what mindful awareness can ease and prevent. Mindfulness training brings more awareness of our outer and inner worlds. For example, when you practise the body scan you learn to become more aware of sensations. You might be surprised to discover areas of tension or that pain can come and go. You might realise that if you notice an itch or a disturbing noise, just observing it may cause less hassle than automatically fighting it and letting it spoil your mood. And then when you practise sitting meditation you find you can deepen the practice of watching your thoughts and emotions rather than getting caught up in them. You may discover a whole hidden landscape of sensations, feelings and thoughts that have been bubbling under the surface. You might be amazed to discover that although you have hardly been aware of them, they have been driving your behaviour in many unhelpful ways. Noticing the features of these hidden landscapes can help you find your way in life more skilfully. It is therefore not surprising that many mindfulness training programmes and online resources aimed at beginners have become so hugely successful.

The mindfulness wave

The mindfulness wave began in the late seventies when Jon Kabat-Zinn developed the Mindfulness-Based Stress Reduction (MBSR) programme at the University of Massachusetts Medical Center.[1] Being both an experienced practitioner of traditional forms of meditation and a scientist in molecular biology, he was in an excellent position to combine teachings from the East with scientific insights from the West. He offered this eight-week course to patients with difficult-to-treat conditions, suffering from chronic pain, ongoing physical restrictions or poor prospects. This training helped them cope better with their stresses, pains and discomforts, even if their diseases could not be cured. Not surprisingly, mindfulness training programmes spread all over the world to be offered wherever people encounter stress. Not only in hospitals and health care settings, also in schools and workplaces, where it could contribute to more well-being, better functioning and prevention of stress-related health hazards and burnout.

Out of MBSR more specific mindfulness-based programmes were developed for people with special kinds of problems, such as Mindfulness-Based Cognitive Therapy (MBCT) for people vulnerable to depression.[2] It can make a world of difference to see your thoughts as just thoughts instead of unshakable truths, especially the negative comments and harsh self-judgments that seem so convincing when you are depressed. Mindfulness not only brings more awareness, it opens the way to becoming kinder to ourselves.

Heartfulness

Without mindfulness, difficult moments can send you skidding around in all directions including up and down on a kind of nightmare roller-coaster with no steering wheel and no brakes. Your instinct is to shut your eyes and scream. Is there something to support you when you are brave enough to open your eyes and mindfully find a way to slow the vehicle down and guide it? At the other extreme, what if it feels like you came to a complete standstill years ago, as if forever stuck on the bleak side of life, deprived of every goodness you once hoped for? Is there anything that could possibly give comfort when you dare to be mindful of your experience then? Fortunately, there is.

That something is 'heartfulness' or compassion. Where mindfulness opens our senses, offering clearer sight and insight, compassion opens our heart, offering a way to relate to the suffering we encounter, however large or small it might be. In fact, mindfulness and compassion cannot be separated. They are like two sides of the same coin or the two wings of a bird. When the inhabitants of that faraway planet taste their raisins in the first session of the mindfulness training, their thoughts will inevitably wander off. Many of them will feel irritated with themselves for not paying attention, but the teacher will remind them to *kindly* bring their minds back to the raisin. A tiny seed of compassion is planted. And just as tiny seeds can grow into huge trees, with practice compassion can grow too. In this book we will offer you many ways of nourishing and developing it and in doing so at the same time deepening your mindfulness practice.

How MBCL began

We began to work with each other from 2007 onwards at the Center for Integrative Psychiatry in the Dutch city of Groningen. Erik, who trained as a Western psychiatrist and psychotherapist, had personally experienced the benefits of meditation and had been teaching mindfulness courses for both clients and professionals. Frits, who had previously lived as a Buddhist monk and worked as a psychiatric nurse, brought in his expertise as a mindfulness trainer and meditation teacher. We got to know each other very well by teaching many out-patient groups and teacher training seminars together. We learned how many participants highly appreciated the refreshing approach and self-healing potential of mindfulness. We also learned that many of them struggled with keeping up the practice and developing a kind and compassionate attitude towards themselves. Many requests came for deepening this work and we felt inspired to develop a follow-on course. This resulted in the Mindfulness-Based Compassionate Living (MBCL) programme. Frits' knowledge of Buddhist psychology and Erik's knowledge of Western science and psychology proved a fruitful combination. The valuable feedback from clients, mindfulness teachers and health care professionals who took part in the courses helped to shape MBCL in the form we offer it now. It has eight sessions to be followed weekly or fortnightly.

The first Dutch book on the course appeared in 2012, followed by German, English and Spanish publications. For the English edition,[3] we were grateful for the generous support from Victoria Norton, who as a native English speaker with ample experience in teaching and communication, assisted us in the writing process. There has been a lot of interest in the MBCL programme and the international demand for lectures, workshops and teacher training seminars has been steadily rising, in health care and other settings. Simultaneously, many others have been working on training and researching compassion and we are very happy to see how the mindfulness wave across the world is being followed by a steadily rising compassion wave.

Based in science

There is a lot of evidence to show that training in compassion is good for our physical and emotional health and helps us have healthier relationships with ourselves and others. MBCL is based on extensive scientific work – pioneered by researchers like Paul Gilbert, Kristin Neff and Barbara Fredrickson – which we summarised in our previous book.[4] Research has shown that people who score high on self-compassion...

- cope better with adversities;
- take more personal initiative and responsibility;
- are less fearful of making mistakes and being rejected;
- have more self-respect, understanding and acceptance of imperfections;
- take better care of themselves by healthier exercising and eating;
- are more emotionally intelligent;
- are happier and more optimistic;
- have more fulfilling relationships.

Several compassion training programmes have been developed that do not require previous mindfulness training, such as the Mindful Self-Compassion programme.[5] MBCL is different, in that we have designed it for people who have already done a mindfulness training. The first studies into MBCL have shown promising results, whether offered as group training for out-patients with mixed psychological problems,[6] or with recurrent depression,[7] or as an online programme for self-referring individuals.[8] Researchers at the Radboud University of Nimwegen in the Netherlands have tested the programme in a larger controlled study with patients suffering from recurrent depression.[9] The included patients had previously participated in MBCT. After completion of the MBCL course they showed a significant increase in mindfulness and self-compassion levels and a decrease in depressive symptoms.[10]

Is MBCL for you?

Feeling stressed and being harsh on ourselves is common among many people, not only in mental health settings, where we originally developed MBCL. The course has therefore been widely offered and much appreciated by clients and professionals from various fields, not only health care, but also education, coaching, pastoral care, management and the workplace.

If you are finding it difficult to cope with the many challenges, threats and distractions of our modern world, you are not alone. Numerous people suffer from stress-related health problems, depression, anxiety, fatigue and burn out and neglect their deeper needs and values. MBCL can be of benefit if you are looking for...

– ways to deal more wisely with the inevitable stresses of life;
– a healthier balance between caring for others and yourself;
– sustainable ways to cultivate more kindness, happiness, health and harmony – in your personal and working lives, in your relationships and in the world at large;
– science-based practices, suitable for people with all kinds of backgrounds.

If you recognise yourself in the above and you are familiar with basic mindfulness practice by having followed MBSR, MBCT, Breathworks or similar courses, the MBCL programme will build on this foundation and deepen your practice. The questions below are offered to reflect on your deeper intentions and motivations for wanting to follow an MBCL course or work through this book by yourself.

Questions for reflection

What do you wish to come out of this training, regarding how you...

– relate to yourself?
– relate to others, such as family, friends, neighbours, colleagues?
– deal with current difficulties in your life?
– engage with other areas in your life that are important to you, such as education and work, health and lifestyle, social activities, nature and spirituality?

continued

> – work towards valuable goals in your life, short term and long term?
> – deal with future challenges?

How to use this book

If this book was recommended to you as part of a group training, you can follow the guidance of the teacher. The eight chapters correspond with the numbers of the eight sessions or classes of the MBCL training. If you are using this book as a self-help guide, we suggest you allow yourself the time it takes to explore the exercises and themes of each chapter rather than reading it from cover to cover straight away.

We normally ask participants to set aside 45 to 60 minutes daily for home practice. Feel free to take one or two weeks per chapter, depending on how much practice time you have. You will find a summary of the session's main themes at the end of each chapter as well as an overview of practice suggestions. Exercises are marked with ※ and offered as framed transcripts in this book and as audio downloads at www.routledge. com/9781138228931. Audios are numbered and marked with an icon ◀⑴ in the text. Downloadable worksheets are also numbered and marked with ▣. Most questions from worksheets you can find in the text in shaded boxes.

In this book we distinguish between formal and informal practices. If you have already started a mindfulness practice, you may have created your own private space where you can do formal practices undisturbed. Just as in the mindfulness courses, the informal practices are done in daily life. Most of the time you do not even have to interrupt your activities to do them. As with all mindfulness practice, you may encounter pleasant and unpleasant experiences. At times you may feel calm, joyful or deeply moved, at other times frustrated, sad or bored. Remember, that there is no 'wrong' experience and simply being mindful of whatever arises is part of the practice. If you notice the pace is too fast, be kind to yourself and slow down. Take time to digest what the exercises stir up. Any time you can return to basic mindfulness practices you already know, like the body scan, sitting meditation or mindful movement. Always feel free to choose whether you do an exercise or not; they are not offered as 'homework', but as 'suggestions for practice'. Depending on how helpful they are, you may practise some exercises more than others. Being kind in what you choose is an important part of developing compassion.

If you are suffering from emotional distress or mental health issues you find difficult to handle, we advise you to seek professional advice. It is important to know that MBCL is not intended to replace therapy. If you are currently in treatment, then it is advisable to talk to the professionals involved and get their approval. The MBCL programme does not offer miracle cures but encourages you to be in charge yourself and be your own therapist. So, you must be ready to trust your own experience in telling you what is helpful and unhelpful in dealing with life's difficulties.

Are you ready to continue the mindful journey and deepen it with compassion practice? If so, we warmly welcome you to join us and hope this book will guide you further on this valuable path. May it contribute to more ease, happiness and wisdom in your life.

Notes

1. Kabat-Zinn, J. (1991). *Full catastrophe living: How to cope with stress, pain and illness using mindfulness meditation.* New York: Dell.
2. Segal, S. V., Williams, J. M. G., & Teasdale, J. D. (2013). *Mindfulness-based cognitive therapy for depression: A new approach to preventing relapse.* New York: Guilford Press.
3. Van den Brink, E. & Koster, F. (2015). *Mindfulness-based compassionate living – A new training programme to deepen mindfulness with heartfulness.* London: Routledge.
4. Chapter 1.6 Research, in: Van den Brink, E. & Koster, F. (2015). *Mindfulness-Based Compassionate Living* (pp. 39–42). London: Routledge. The three researchers mentioned have accessibly written about their work for non-professional readers: Gilbert, P. (2009). *The compassionate mind.* London: Constable and Robinson; Neff, K. (2011). *Self-compassion.* New York: HarperCollins; Fredrickson, B. L. (2013). *Love 2.0.* New York: Penguin.
5. Neff, K. D., & Germer, C. K. (2012). A pilot study and randomized controlled trial of the mindful self-compassion program. *Journal of Clinical Psychology, 69,* 28–44.
6. Bartels-Velthuis, A. A., Schroevers, M. J., Ploeg, K. van der, Koster, F., Fleer, J. & Brink, E. van den (2016). A Mindfulness-Based Compassionate Living training in a heterogeneous sample of psychiatric outpatients: A feasibility study. *Mindfulness, 7,* 809–818.
7. Schuling, R., Huijbers, M., Jansen, H., Metzemaekers, R., Van den Brink, E., Koster, F., Van Ravesteijn, H. & Speckens, A. (2018). The co-creation and feasibility of a compassion training as a follow-up to Mindfulness Based Cognitive Therapy in patients with recurrent depression. *Mindfulness, 9,* 412–422.
8. Krieger, T., Martig, D.S., Brink, E. van den, & Berger, T. (2016). Working on self-compassion online: A roof of concept and feasibility Study. *Internet Interventions, 6,* 64–70.
9. Schuling, R., Huijbers, M. J., van Ravesteijn, H., Donders, R., Kuyken, W., & Speckens, A. E. M. (2016). A parallel-group, randomized controlled trial into the effectiveness of Mindfulness-Based Compassionate Living (MBCL) compared to treatment-as-usual in recurrent depression: Trial design and protocol. *Contemporary Clinical Trials, 50,* 77–83.
10. Schuling, R., Huijbers, M. J., Van Ravesteijn, H., Donders, R., Kuyken, W. & A. E. M. Speckens (submitted February 2018). Effectiveness of Mindfulness-Based Compassionate Living compared with treatment-as-usual in recurrent depression: An RCT. *Journal of Clinical and Consulting Psychology.*

Chapter 1

Wired to survive rather than thrive

Session one: how we evolved – threat, drive and soothing systems

Life is simple, it's just not easy.

—Unknown source

Being human is a challenge

Being human is a big mystery. It is as if we wake up one day, finding ourselves thrown into this life, realising we are a human being. We start off by not choosing to be here and then we are continually confronted by circumstances that were not our choice either. We did not choose where we came from and how evolution shaped us. We are an ongoing work in progress, trying to adapt to life's ever-changing challenges, not knowing where we are going. Even if you were lucky enough to have a fair start and were raised in a warm and loving family, in relatively peaceful and prosperous circumstances, you will sooner or later encounter difficulties, smaller or bigger traumas, frustrations and losses. Even if you feel fine at the moment, you know you are going to grow old and die and eventually lose all that is dear to you. The world is impermanent, largely uncontrollable and practically unpredictable.

All this may not sound very cheerful but bear with us a little longer. This is exactly where compassion begins. When we realise suffering is inevitable because we live in an imperfect body, in an imperfect world, with many others who are just as imperfect as we are, compassion is not a luxury but a basic need.

Compassion: not for the faint-hearted

So, why is it so difficult to be compassionate? To explore this, reflect a while on the following question: Why would you *not* practise compassion towards yourself?

When we ask participants in a training course, they often tell us things like:

- I will have to invest time and energy in something that might not even help.
- It might stir up pain and sorrow.
- I do not deserve it.
- I might become selfish or lazy.
- There are so many people in this world who need it more than I do.
- I was raised to be firm with myself. I do not want to become a wimp.
- What on earth would my mates at the football club think?

There may also be arguments not to practise compassion towards others, such as:

- I am already exhausted from looking after others' needs.
- There is so much suffering in this world. It makes me feel so helpless.
- Why should I feel compassion for people who hurt me?
- How can you be compassionate with dictators and terrorists?

We like to get these ideas and biases about compassion into the open, because they are common and fully understandable. We will not give them a lot of discussion however, because clarity about these issues will more likely come from your own experience of the practices offered in this course rather than from discussion. It may be good, however, to offer a concise definition of compassion. Having researched compassion for decades, Paul Gilbert[1] defines compassion as

1   a sensitivity to suffering in *ourselves and others* (it goes both ways!); and
2   a commitment to try to alleviate and prevent it.

So, compassion is definitely not for the faint-hearted. It has a receptive and tender side, but also an active and powerful side. Clearly, it involves courage to face our suffering and deal with it as best as we can. On the other hand, it is not about jumping into the deep end when you cannot swim. Compassion also needs wisdom and patience. We certainly do not want you to feel pressurised to become compassionate, neither with yourself nor with others. Just try the exercises you feel ready to do and mindfully observe what happens while you do them.

It may reassure you to know that scientific evidence is piling up that compassion not only alleviates suffering, it also contributes to happiness, and, like mindfulness, you can cultivate it with practice.[2] So, we would like to start with a brief exercise, which you can do any time during the day when it is safe to pause. It is derived from the Three Minute Breathing Space known from MBCT[3] combined with the practice of Soothing Breathing Rhythm, which is a basic exercise in Compassion Focused

Therapy.[4] It consists of three phases which, of course, may be longer or shorter than one minute each.

※ BREATHING SPACE WITH KINDNESS

1 Open, kind awareness

Find a comfortable position, either sitting, lying or standing ... noticing what you are experiencing right now ... thoughts, feelings, physical sensations, or sounds ... kindly acknowledging whatever arises, the pleasant and the unpleasant ... welcoming all experiences, just as they present themselves.

2 Focus on the breath and allowing a soothing breathing rhythm

Then let your attention rest on the breath, following every in- and out-breath with relaxed attention. Allow a calming, soothing breathing rhythm to emerge by gently slowing down and deepening the movements of the breath. Allow the out-breath to flow out all the way, until the direction of flow changes by itself. Let the body fill on the in-breath, until the next out-breath naturally follows. A soothing breathing rhythm may be supported by consciously sensing the ground that supports you, allowing your muscles and face to soften, your chest and heart to open like a flower towards the light, your belly to freely rise and fall ... If you like, kindly placing one or both hands on the body. When the breath has found its soothing rhythm, you can just let it follow its own course. Be kind when you realise your mind has drifted off. It is what minds normally do. As soon as you notice this, mindfulness has returned. Acknowledge what is there right now. Gently guide your attention back to the breath, and if you lose the soothing rhythm, allow it to return.

3 Whole body awareness and offering a kind wish

Then expand your awareness to the body as a whole, the breathing body as it sits, lies or stands here. Tune into yourself and notice what comes up when you ask yourself: 'What could be a kind, supportive wish to myself right now? For instance, 'May I feel safe' ... or 'May I feel healthy ... happy ... at ease'. Choose the words that come from your heart and that can be taken to heart ... If you like you can allow this wish to flow through you on the rhythm of the breath. For instance, 'May I...' on the in-breath and '... feel safe' on the out-breath. Repeat the whole phrase or just one or two keywords and mindfully acknowledge what arises while you let this kind wish flow through you. A gentle smile may accompany the offering of the wish, like you would also do when you give a present to another person. Feeling the touch of one or both hands on your heart may support your receiving of the wish. Every experience, pleasant or unpleasant, can be welcomed as part of the practice. You may end this exercise when you wish and return to it whenever you find a good moment.

The human brain and its flaws

The human brain changes with experience like no other organ, enabling us to learn from and adapt to varying circumstances. Evolution scientists view the human brain as a complex survival organ with properties dating back to prehistoric times, long before humans ever existed. Evolution is such a slow process that our bodies and brains always fall behind in their ability to handle new circumstances and new situations. We are, for instance, not designed to eat fast food, sit nonstop behind computer screens, and keep up 24/7 with messages from social media and smartphones. Still, this is what many of us do every day. The design of our brains and bodies was shaped when we lived in caves as hunter gatherers, protecting ourselves from predators. Although we may live longer nowadays, we are not necessarily healthier and happier. There are gross mismatches between our nature and our culture, between the design of our brain and body and our modern lifestyles and rapidly changing world.

The brain is thought to have evolved into a multi-layered organ.[5] Figure 1.1 illustrates the main layers:

– The *reptilian brain* or *brainstem* is the oldest part, with an estimated history of 500 million years, enabling largely automatic reactions for basic survival, such as escaping threat, hunting prey, digesting food and mating.
– The *old mammalian* or *emotional brain* evolved in mammals some 200 million years ago, when living in groups became crucial for survival. It enables emotional processes important for social bonding, working out rank and status, and giving and receiving care.
– The *new mammalian brain,* simply *new brain,* or *neocortex,* the youngest and most changeable part, evolved 'just' 2 million years ago, when our ancestors 'got smart' and adapted to ever more complex societies. It enables imagery, reason and language, memory and planning, worry and fantasy, art and science.

Taken together, the reptilian brain and emotional brain are called the *old brain*. The old brain reacts fast to information received from the senses. These reactions are largely instinctual and automatic, guided by what feels

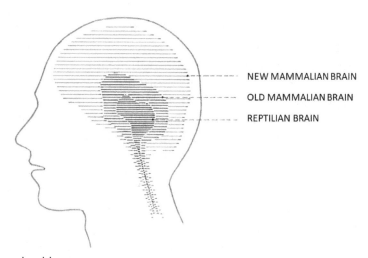

NEW MAMMALIAN BRAIN

OLD MAMMALIAN BRAIN

REPTILIAN BRAIN

Figure 1.1 The evolved brain

pleasant or unpleasant, along fast neural circuits, often referred to as the *short route* or *low road*. On the other hand, the new brain is slower. It processes sensory information and emotional responses through reflection and reasoning, which takes time. Therefore, it is called the *long route* or *high road*. To complicate matters, new brain activity can set off old brain reactions and vice versa. For example, our new brains enable us to catastrophise about a minor mistake we made at work, putting the old brain into a state of alarm and making us irritable with our loved ones at home. Regular neural traffic between old and new brains can create spirals or *loops* leading to healthy and unhealthy habits. Unfortunately, unhealthy habits exacerbate the inevitable suffering we already have on our plates.

Like Pandora's box

You may know the story of Pandora from ancient Greece.[6] Zeus, the king of the gods, was furious with man because Prometheus had stolen the secret of fire from him. Out of revenge he sent Pandora to earth and gave her a jar – in later versions a box – containing everything terrible you can possibly imagine. She did not know what was inside and was told under no condition to open it. But Pandora was very curious and you can guess what happened. Rather incautiously, she opened the jar and before she could close it, all the evils escaped and spread like a plague across humanity.

When you know about the old brain and the new brain you can start to understand why we can be very impulsive and emotional as well as highly rational. Both parts are important, but they can influence each other in unpredictable ways and the human brain can be as surprising as Pandora's box. If you cross the street and suddenly a car comes round the corner, your old brain reaction to jump out of the way would save your life. Waiting for a slow and intelligent new brain response to come up would be fatal. But blindly following your old brain reactions can lead to disaster in other situations. If you impulsively shout insults at your boss and slam doors at work, you could ruin a relationship that took years to establish. Pausing for a moment to make use of your new brain to reflect before you act might save you from being sacked.

New brain functions can easily be taken over by old brain processes. Consider the troubles in the world where despotic leaders let their new brains become driven by primitive old brain motives. Vice versa, new brain processes can trigger unhealthy old brain reactions. A rabbit losing a carrot to a larger and more brazen rabbit would not blame itself for failing or worry itself sick about ever getting another carrot. But we humans can blame ourselves into depression and catastrophise, panic and despair. Of course, our new brains can be a blessing. They enable us to solve complex problems and use science and art to bring more happiness and harmony into the world. But they can also be a curse, enabling us to make our lives miserable by simply imagining what went wrong, is wrong or could go wrong. What we construct in our minds with the help of our new brains can be so powerful that we can create heaven or hell on earth.

Just knowing that *the design of our brain is not of our making and there-fore not our fault* can be a good starting point to be compassionate with ourselves. You probably would not blame yourself for bodily flaws, such as poor eyesight, moles on your skin, or a predisposition to low back pain. So why blame yourself for a tricky brain?

Insight: the good fairy

It might not be our fault how the brain is designed, but we do have a responsibility to deal with it wisely. The encouraging part in children's versions of Pandora's story is that she shut the box just in time to catch the good fairy. She was called Hope, but we can also see her as a metaphor for 'insight'. Insight arises from observing and under-standing our inner processes. Although there are all sorts of unfortu-nate loops of old and new brain interactions, we can at least begin to see them. Insight is enabled by the newest parts of our brain, roughly the area of the medial forebrain, which has been referred to as *the mindful brain.*[7] It is estimated to have emerged 'only' 10,000 years ago. This part is like Pandora's good fairy, because when we use our mindful brain to observe our thoughts, feelings and bodily sensa-tions, we become less driven by 'evils' and more capable of respond-ing wisely to life's challenges.

Like no other animal on this planet, we have the potential to be boundlessly cruel or boundlessly compassionate. By training the capacity to observe our inner processes with openness and kindness, we can grad-ually evolve into mindful compassionate human beings.

Three emotion regulation systems

Now, let us have a closer look at the old brain processes of emotion regulation. From the point of evolutionary psychology, emotions function as messengers who have our best interests at heart. They motivate us to survive and live as comfortably as possible, even if they feel unpleasant. The oldest emotions scream loudly when there is danger or when there are basic needs to be met. When our imme-diate survival is secure, we may hear the subtle whispers of younger messengers, informing us whether we are moving in the direction of more sustainable happiness and harmony. Based on Paul Gilbert's work, we will share with you a model of three basic systems for emo-tion regulation and motivation.[8] With a little practice, you can rec-ognise their different qualities in your own life, but to get the idea it might be easier to think of a cat (*Figure 1.2*).

As the three systems are very helpful in understanding our own behaviour and recognising the old-brain-animal inside us, we discuss them in more detail below. You will find a more schematic model in Figure 1.3.

The cat

*The three basic emotion regulation systems can be easily observed in a cat. If a cat feels secure, she might lie down in the garden and relax in the sun. If there is nothing in particular to be done, her attention wanders unfocused. She may purr when stroked, play with a kitten, or nod off. She is in her **soothing system** and rests.*

*If a barking dog suddenly appears, she jumps up with arched back and fluffed tail, hissing at the intruder. Immediately, her **threat system** is switched on. Her body is all tense and her attention is narrowly focused on what she does not want, which is this offensive dog. She might try and scratch it or run off, depending on its size. When she feels safe again, it does not take long until she returns to her soothing system. Now, we humans often need much longer to return to the soothing system, as we will very easily start imagining what could have gone wrong or what might go wrong if the dog returns. But the cat is untroubled by this. She relaxes again and, if not sleepy, may play around with open attention for her surroundings.*

*If the cat feels hungry and sees a mouse, she is suddenly on alert again and her muscles tense up. Now we recognise the energy of the **drive system**, which is different from the threat system. She is driven toward the object of her desire and her attention focuses on what she wants, which is to catch this mouse. If she is successful, she will fill her stomach. She will not be bothered by human thoughts about getting more than she actually needs and will soon happily surrender to her soothing system again.*

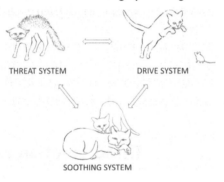

THREAT SYSTEM DRIVE SYSTEM

SOOTHING SYSTEM

Figure 1.2 The three systems in a cat

The threat system

In order to survive, we first need to protect ourselves from danger. So, this system is the most fundamental. When it is active our attention is narrowly focused on *what we don't want*, which is what threatens us. The emotions fear, aversion and aggression feel unpleasant so we feel alarmed and urgently look for safety. There may be different reactions to threat. If our enemy looks beatable, or if we are trapped and have no choice we *fight*. If the enemy looks too strong our reaction is *flight*. The enemy might overlook us when we *freeze* or be fooled into thinking we are dead when we *faint*. Nowadays, trauma specialists also distinguish two other stress reactions from the threat system.[9] When escaping from outer threat seems impossible, we may react with *submission*, like a dog lying on its back when the opponent is too strong. Or we may react with *dissociation*, which is like switching off consciousness to protect ourselves from inner pain.

The drive system

This system is directed towards getting what we need to survive. We focus our attention on *what we want*. We are after rewards such as food, sexual partners, pleasure, success, power or possessions. The object of our desire can be material or immaterial. The emotions excitement, arousal, pleasure and satisfaction are predominantly pleasant but do not last long. We strive, compete, achieve, consume. When we do not get what we want, we become easily frustrated and envious of those who are more successful.

The soothing system

This system supports calming down and social bonding and can come on stage when dangers have passed and needs are fulfilled. If there are no immediate *wants* or *don't wants*, our awareness becomes spacious. The emotional state of calmness, contentment, safeness and connectedness feels pleasant and has a more soothing and sustainable quality than the pleasant emotions of the drive system.[10] Our behaviour is kind, caring and playful. Paul Gilbert deliberately uses the word 'safeness' here, which is a very different state to be in than the 'safety' sought by the threat system. An air raid shelter offers physical safety, whereas a warm cosy home offers also emotional safeness.

The stress of threat and drive

Whenever we are in our threat or drive systems the stress levels are usually quite high. Our nervous system and stress hormones create a

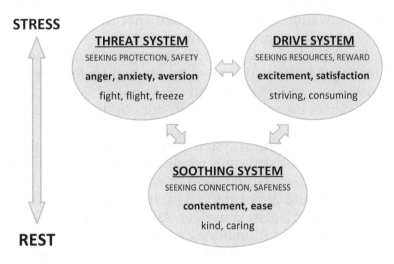

Figure 1.3 The three systems in balance[11]

state of arousal, alerting our attention towards what we need to avoid or need to catch. The breathing rhythm and heart rate accelerate, the blood pressure rises. The muscles tense up and receive more blood, while the digestive and immune systems tune down and receive less, as they are not vital for immediate survival. These systems consume a lot of energy and were designed for brief bursts of activity to escape from danger or hunt for food. It can lead to exhaustion if we stay in them for too long. In the mindfulness course, we learn about the 'doing mode', which can have the energy of the threat or the drive system. Think about a farmer who tries to make his donkey work for him. Both punishment and reward may do the trick. He can get the donkey to move by threatening it with a stick from behind or luring it by dangling a carrot in front. The carrot might be more effective, but being too long in either the drive or threat system will eventually stress and frustrate the animal. If it were free to choose, the donkey would prefer to graze peacefully in the meadow with other donkeys, in the relaxed 'being mode' of the soothing system.

Rest and digest

Animals naturally sense what is needed to keep a healthy balance. Whenever they can, they gravitate into the soothing system. Then the breathing rhythm and the heart rate slow down, the blood pressure falls and the muscles relax, allowing the digestive and immune systems to become active. This relaxed state allows for recovery, nourishment and growth, and is referred to as *rest and digest* (as opposed to fight and flight). Reptiles have plenty of offspring so they do not need to be prosocial. However, mammals have limited offspring and their survival depends on taking care of each other, particularly of their vulnerable young ones. So, social bonding and attachment became crucial in mammalian life and the rest and digest state expanded with the warm emotional tone of feeling soothed and connected. The newer branches of the vagus or 'wandering' nerve helped that to happen.[12] This nerve represents the calming part of the nervous system and it connects the emotional brain with many internal organs, especially the heart. The soothing feeling is further supported by the brain releasing natural opiate-like substances (endorphins) and the so-called 'love hormone' oxytocin, which causes the warm feeling in our chest when we feel socially connected.[13]

So, the emotion regulation systems are important in motivating us to move away from what harms and move toward what supports us. If we had no threat system, we would soon be run over by a car. If we had no drive system, we would die of starvation. If we had no soothing system, we would exhaust and isolate ourselves. All three contribute in their own way to survival. However, humans are complex beings and do not always have the healthy balance between these systems as suggested in *Figure 1.3*. In the following exercise, we invite you to reflect on this.

※ CONTEMPLATING THE THREE SYSTEMS IN YOUR LIFE

Consider how the three emotion regulation systems have developed in your own life. Draw the threat, drive and soothing systems as three circles on a sheet of paper, similar to Figure 1.2, but draw a bigger circle for the stronger system and a smaller circle for the weaker one.

How are you going to decide how big to draw the circles? Well, think of the amount of activation (intended or unintended) each system has had in your past and current life. Reflect on the following questions. They may be difficult to answer. Just notice with kind attention what comes up, without force, even if what comes up is painful. If nothing comes up, that's fine too. You can write keywords in the circles. Be gentle with yourself. You can always allow for a pause and return to the exercise later.

- *What experiences, circumstances, persons were important in shaping your threat, drive and soothing systems?*
- *What were you afraid of? What did you long for? What did you need the most?*
- *Which survival or coping strategies did you develop? Some strategies may be outwardly directed, such as avoiding others, pleasing others or competing with others. Other strategies may be inwardly directed, such as avoiding painful emotions, clinging to pleasant feelings, criticising yourself or striving for perfection.*
- *What are unintended consequences of these strategies?*
- *What does this tell you and what would be a kind wish to yourself?*

You can end this reflection by allowing a soothing breathing rhythm and repeating the kind wish that came up with the last question. Gently letting this wish flow through you, e.g. 'May I...' on the in-breath and 'feel safe ... connected ... at ease...' on the out-breath.

Getting out of balance

We have met very few participants in our courses who considered their soothing system circle to be over-sized. However, there are plenty who feel that the other two systems are over-developed. Unlike other animals, we keep these energy-intensive threat and drive systems going for much longer than they are designed for by evolution. We seem to be better at generating stress than at getting rest.

Quite often, we find ourselves avoiding sticks or chasing carrots in our imaginations! So, even when we appear to be resting, we are actually in 'doing mode'. It proved an evolutionary advantage that we became better at learning from our past and avoiding mistakes in the future. So, understandably, we do a lot of looking back and projecting forward. But there is a downside if our threat and drive systems are continually being activated by ruminations on the past, worries about the future, fantasies about what we need to be happy, or fears of what others think of us. These threat and drive programmes seem so hardwired in our brains that they often run the show and drain our energy.

Avoiding sticks

Have you ever wondered why our news bulletins are crammed with negative events? Our tendency to be drawn to possible threats and remember what was harmful, is called the 'negativity bias'.[14] Apparently, we have a permanently active radar for spotting possible danger. And if only once a danger proves real, we never forget it. Rick Hanson used the comparison that our memory is like Velcro for the negative but has a Teflon layer for the positive.[15] It is no surprise that the threat system easily dominates the other systems. It is the default mode of the old brain.

Chasing carrots

When resources were scarce we needed to grab what we could to survive. However, in modern times and in developed countries this can lead to unhealthy greed, consumerism and the exhaustion of global resources. Given the emphasis our culture puts on individual achievement, competitiveness and gaining wealth and success, it is no wonder our drive systems work overtime. We easily become addicted to all sorts of wants, haves and pleasures and our self-esteem depends on it. Nowadays, this is strongly enforced by social media and the number of contacts, 'followers' and 'likes' we get.

So, on the one hand, we are fearful of loss and inferiority and on the other hand we are striving for gain and superiority. We spend a lot of time being battered back and forth between our threat and drive systems and we neglect our soothing system. Not surprisingly, this creates all kinds of stress-related health problems. So, how do we create a healthier balance?

Restoring the balance

You already made a start with the first exercise. Allowing a soothing breathing rhythm increases the vagal tone and a healthy heart rate variability, calming our emotional brains. Making a kind gesture by putting a hand on the heart area can, in the right circumstances, support the release of oxytocin and feelings of warmth, openness and connection. By nourishing the soothing system, we empower the 'low road' to compassion,[16] bringing our old brains and bodies in line to receive and give kindness and care. We can also practise the 'high road' by working with mindfulness and compassionate imagery, training our new brains to create better conditions for the soothing system.

Thus, we train our old and new brains to form positive loops and upward spirals of physical, psychological and social well-being, creating more resilience to stress.[17]

Just as we become more physically fit by exercising the muscles of our body, we can create more mental balance by practising mindfulness and compassion. We train our brain by walking both the high and low roads towards compassion. So, here is an exercise where you are invited to use your imagination in a playful way.

※ A SAFE PLACE

As a start of any exercise, you can always begin with the first two steps of Breathing Space with Kindness, as described in the first exercise. Also, when you feel stuck, you can remind yourself of simply being mindful of whatever arises and reconnect with a soothing breathing rhythm. You can gently resume the exercise when you feel ready to do so.

Now imagine yourself being at a place where you can feel secure and at ease, a safe place where you can be peacefully alone, just the way you are, without anybody else around. Exercises with others will follow later in the training. It may be a place coming up from memory or fantasy, or both ... It can be a place outdoors, at the seaside, in a forest or garden ... or indoors in a cosy corner of your home ... or anywhere.

What does your place look like? Does a visual image emerge? ... What shapes, what colours do you see? If there is no clear visual image, that's fine too. Perhaps your imagination reveals what your other senses would notice at a safe place? What sounds? What fragrances? How does the contact with the surroundings feel? Do you feel warmth or coolness? A particular touch or support? It may be just a subtle sense of an atmosphere of safeness. Observe the details of your experience.

Images can be fleeting, or different places pass by. That's fine. It is how our minds work. Just acknowledging what arises. There is no wrong experience. This exercise is at the same time a practice in mindfulness. All experiences can be welcomed with playful curiosity; and every response to what you experience, pleasant or unpleasant, can be noticed with a non-judgmental mind. Just imagine the safe place welcoming you with whatever experience you may have.

What sensations arise in the body when you imagine yourself in this safe place? How do your muscles feel, your face, chest, belly? What feelings and thoughts do you notice?

Now imagine the place really appreciates your presence, however you feel. That it finds joy in welcoming you and wishes you well ... How does that affect you?

Continue as long as you wish, knowing you can always return to this practice, wherever you are and however you feel. At any time, you can practise imagining a place to come home to, again and again, in whatever form it will reveal itself.

If you wish, you can make short notes on your experience of this exercise on the worksheet, guided by the following questions.

Questions for reflection

– Which place(s) arose during the exercise?
– Which senses were you most aware of during the exercise?
– Which bodily sensations, feelings and thoughts did you observe?
– What was it like to imagine that the place really appreciated you were there?
– What are you noticing now, while reflecting on the practice?
– What could be a kind wish to yourself?

Another way to train our brain is derived from the traditional practice of Loving Kindness Meditation.[18] Here, we present it in a contemporary way. As with mindfulness practice you do not need to follow a particular tradition to practice kindness. We will gradually expand this practice in the weeks to come. We start with offering kindness to the person you deal with most of all in your life ... Yes, yourself.

※ KINDNESS MEDITATION: YOURSELF

Sit down comfortably on a chair a cushion or meditation bench ... in an upright position, with relaxed attention ... If you have physical limitations, you can, of course, adjust your position or lie down, at any time. Here again, begin the practice with the first two steps of Breathing Space with Kindness, and you can return to these again and again ... Allow yourself to arrive in the moment, mindfully welcoming whatever arises ... gently allow the breath to soften and deepen, until a soothing rhythm emerges ... Then let the breath flow by itself...

If you wish, you can first connect with the atmosphere of kindness by letting a memory come to mind of an experience when you felt kindly welcomed and at ease, and your heart was filled with feelings of joy, contentment and gratitude. Allow the memory to come alive vividly by inviting all senses involved: What was there to see, hear, smell, feel ... How does this affect you now, in your body, heart and mind?

From this sense of kindness, you are invited to repeat a wish to yourself. What could be a kind wish that connects well with you? What could be a wish from the heart? Allow yourself to be surprised. Perhaps a wish will spontaneously arise ... If not, you can use one of four traditional phrases that are generally deep needs of us all: 'May I feel safe...' 'May I feel healthy...' 'May I feel happy...' or 'May I feel at ease.'

Phrases like this can flow with the breath if you wish. The first part 'May I...' or 'I wish myself...' with the in-breath and the second part with the out-breath. Let the words flow through your body and your whole being, sensing the giving and receiving side. The giving aspect can be encouraged by consciously allowing a soft face and a gentle smile; the receiving aspect by touching your heart area with one or both hands, supporting the intention to take the wish to heart. If this does not feel right, you may wish to explore whether touching the body elsewhere feels soothing. Do not hesitate to change the phrase into words you find you can more easily receive. The practice is not about getting what you want. You cannot force the wish to come true. It is not about making up good feelings but about cultivating goodwill towards yourself. After a while, you may just repeat a keyword, such as 'safe', 'happy', 'calm' or 'contented', on the rhythm of the breath or independent from it. If words like 'health' or 'happiness' seem too far-fetched, then 'as healthy as can be' or 'May I be strong ... have courage ... be patient ... feel supported' may be more appropriate. Allow the wish to flow through you like a healing energy.

Whatever you experience, joy or sadness, feeling touched or resistant, energised or fatigued, mindfully acknowledge whatever is there. It is all part of the practice. There are no wrong experiences. Any time you find yourself caught in reactions or distractions, is an opportunity to be present with whatever shows itself, welcoming it with an open mind; if need be, allowing a soothing breathing rhythm to return. And if there is space again, return to repeating the kind wishes.

Sometimes, if you notice you are fighting particular experiences, a paradoxical wish can be just as kind. For instance, 'Let me feel this tiredness ... this anger ... this sadness ... just as it is.'

Continue this practice of kindness towards yourself as long as you wish.

You can make notes on this exercise on Worksheet 4.

Questions for reflection

- What wish(es) connected most with you?
- Which physical sensations did you notice while you practised?
- Which thoughts and feelings did you observe?
- What was noticeable in the giving and the receiving of the wish(es)?
- What are you noticing now, while reflecting on the practice?
- What could be a kind wish now?

Suiting your soothing system

As already pointed out, we generally do not need to feed our threat and drive systems, as they are powerful enough already. During meditation practice, you can often observe their activity, also in more subtle ways. For instance, if you begin to worry or experience resistance, the threat system is switched on. If you work hard to be really good at the practice or strive for a good experience, the drive system will be triggered. If you mindfully and compassionately notice the energies of these systems, rather than fighting them, you have already allowed some space for the soothing system to return. Here are a number of other ways to consciously support and nourish the soothing system:

- Music can strongly influence our emotional states. Discover for yourself which music has a soothing effect on you, either by listening, singing or playing an instrument, if you have one. Which sounds, melodies or rhythms strike the compassion-chord in you and enable a soothing breathing rhythm? Allow room for yet unknown possibilities.

– Some people resonate more with rhythm and sound, others more with colour and shape. Which colours have a calming effect or fill you with warmth, kindness, gentleness or courage? You can playfully imagine inhaling a colour, letting it spread throughout your body. How does it make you feel, while you imagine this? You can also look around in nature for colours and shapes that evoke feelings of kindness and ease, or creatively explore by drawing, painting or photography.

– Touch is a very basic sense for conveying soothing and safeness. Think of the comfort a child finds in carrying a soft object, such as a teddy bear. Explore what qualities of touch or being touched make you feel at ease. You may regularly treat yourself to a self-massage or gently and rhythmically tap the body with your hands and fingers. Also, trauma-experts recommend this as a self-soothing practice.[19]

– Similarly, you can explore smelling and tasting, real or imagined. You can imagine inhaling a soothing fragrance and let it spread through you. Of course, we do not wish you to fall into the trap of comfort-eating, but you can mindfully explore the soothing effect of taste while you eat your everyday food.

– You may wish to collect objects, texts or poems that inspire you with kindness, joy and compassion. You can place them around you when you do your practices.

Of course, all these suggestions do not have to be explored immediately. Allow yourself time in the weeks to come to playfully discover how the soothing system can be nourished. Feel invited to mindfully and heartfully come home to your senses, also by regularly doing the next exercise.

※ A PLEASURE WALK

Treat yourself to a walk, if possible in natural surroundings; or anywhere where you can feel at ease. Find yourself a soothing walking rhythm, that eases the state of your body and mind. It does not need to be very slow and may be variable, depending on outer and inner weather conditions. Allow a soft face and gentle smile, let the breath flow freely while you walk.

Open your heart and your senses to explore what arises in and around you, particularly anything that gives a pleasant feeling tone. Are there any soothing sensations to notice in or at the surface of your body: perhaps feeling the strength and relaxation in your muscles, solid ground under your feet, a soft breeze through your hair, the warm rays of the sun on your skin. If something beautiful, joyful or touching draws your attention from the surroundings, allow yourself to pause and mindfully explore what it is: a fragrance that you smell, the beauty of a flower, the shape of a tree, the movement of the clouds, the expression of people's faces, the colours of their clothes, the singing of a bird, sounds of playing children, reflections in the water ... Explore the details as well as sensing the overall atmosphere. Take your time to let it sink in … noticing how the body responds.

Then, resume your soothing walking rhythm until the next invitation to pause … exploring what it actually is that reveals its beauty, evokes feelings of joy, fills you with gratitude … Also, thoughts, associations and images in your mind arising during your walk, can be sources of joy. For instance, even when it rains you may feel gratitude thinking of the many creatures in nature that benefit from the rain.

Many people find it helpful during mindfulness and compassion training to take notes, either in a diary or with the help of worksheets you can download. Formulating experiences and observations in words can be an extra source of insight. We also offer calendar exercises with a different theme for each week. This can aid informal practice by drawing your attention to events when they spontaneously arise in everyday life.

※ Calendar: Soothing System

This week the invitation is to reflect daily on an experience of the soothing system that occurred that day. You can make notes on Worksheet 5 guided by the following questions. We recommend you do this soon after the actual experience, when your memory of it is still vivid.

Questions for reflection

- What was the situation?
- How and when did you become aware of the soothing system?
- Which bodily experiences did you notice?
- Which thoughts and feelings did you notice?
- What are you noticing right now, while reflecting on the experience?
- What could be a kind wish to yourself?

SUMMARY CHAPTER 1

In the first chapter, we pay attention to the 'why' of training compassion and link it to the scientific understanding of how human beings were shaped by evolution. Without fault of our own the imperfect design of our brain can give rise to a lot of suffering. We explain three basic systems of emotion regulation – the threat, drive and soothing systems. Our threat and drive systems easily become overactive at the expense of our soothing system. This imbalance can result in many stress-related health problems. Compassion practice can help restore the balance.

continued

SUGGESTIONS FOR PRACTICE

Formal

- Contemplate The Three Systems in Your Own Life (p. 17).
- Regularly do the exercise a Safe Place. 🔊 📝
- Regularly practise Kindness Meditation towards yourself. 🔊 📝
- Explore what may help support your soothing system and regularly take a Pleasure Walk (p. 22).

Informal

- Do regularly, for instance twice daily in between your daily activities, the Breathing Space with Kindness. 🔊
- Calendar: Soothing System. 📝

You can download general worksheets for keeping notes during the course week by week. 📝

Notes

1. Gilbert, P. (2017). Compassion: Definitions and controversies. In P. Gilbert (ed.), *Compassion – concepts, research and applications* (pp. 3–15). London: Routledge.
2. Summarised in Chapter 1.6 Research in: Van den Brink, E. & Koster, F. (2015). *Mindfulness-based compassionate living* (pp. 30–42). London: Routledge.
3. Segal, S. V., Williams, J. M. G., & Teasdale, J. D. (2013). *Mindfulness-based cognitive therapy for depression: A new approach to preventing relapse.* New York: Guilford Press.
4. Gilbert, P. (2010). *Compassion focused therapy.* London: Routledge.
5. MacLean, P. D. (1990). *The triune brain in evolution: Role in paleocerebral functions.* New York: Springer. Accessible introductions into the evolution of the human brain can be found in: Hanson, R. (2009), with Mendius, R., *Buddha's brain: The practical neuroscience of happiness, love & wisdom.* Oakland, CA: New Harbinger Publications; Hanson, R. (2013). *Hardwiring happiness: The new brain science of contentment, calm, and confidence.* New York: Harmony.
6. https://en.wikipedia.org/wiki/Pandora; accessed 30 June 2017.
7. Siegel, D. J. (2007); *The mindful brain: Reflection and attunement in the cultivation of well-being.* New York: W.W. Norton.
8. Gilbert, P. (2009). *The compassionate mind.* London: Constable & Robinson.
9. Lee, D., & James, S. (2012). *The compassionate mind approach to recovering from trauma.* London: Constable & Robinson.
10. Depue, R. A., & Morrone-Strupinsky, J. V. (2005). A neurobehavioral mod-

el of affiliative bonding. *Behavioral and Brain Sciences, 28,* 313–395.

11. For didactic purposes we use a simplified diagram, which is derived from Gilbert, P. (2009). *The compassionate mind* (p. 22). London: Constable & Robinson. We place the soothing system at the bottom, as explained in: Van den Brink, E. & Koster, F. (2015). *Mindfulness-based compassionate living* (p. 55). London: Routledge.

12. Porges, S. W. (2007). The polyvagal perspective. *Biological Psychology, 74,* 116–143.

13. Olff, M., Frijling, J. L., Kubzansky, L. D., Bradley, B., Ellenbogen, M. A., Cardoso, C., Bartz, J. A., Yee, J. R. & Van Zuiden, M. (2013). The role of oxytocin in social bonding, stress regulation and mental health: An update on the moderating effects of context and interindividual differences. *Psychoneuroendocrinology, 38,* 1883–1894.

14. Rozin, P., & Royzman, E. B. (2001). Negativity bias, negativity dominance, and contagion. *Personality and Social Psychology Review, 5,* 296–320.

15. Hanson, R. (2013). *Hardwiring happiness.* New York: Harmony.

16. Goleman, D. (2006). *Social intelligence: The new science of human relationships.* New York: Bantam.

17. Kok, B. E., Coffey, K. A., Colm, M. A., Catalino, L. I., Vacharkulksemsuk, T., Algoe, S. B., Brantley, M. & Fredrickson, B. L. (2013). How positive emotions build physical health: Perceived positive social connections account for the upward spiral between positive emotions and vagal tone. *Psychological Science, 24,* 1123–1132.

18. Salzberg, S. (1995). *Loving-kindness: The revolutionary art of happiness.* Boston: Shambhala.

19. Van der Kolk, B. (2014). *The body keeps the score.* New York: Penguin.

Chapter 2

Embracing inner demons

Session two: threat and self-compassion

*The true voyage of discovery is not in seeking new land-
scapes but in having new eyes.*

—Marcel Proust[1]

Exploring inner landscapes

Long ago, explorers set out to discover new parts of the world. They
embarked on their journeys not knowing what they would find. They
needed a good dose of courage and curiosity if they were going to make
new discoveries. There were no maps, so they needed an open mind and
willingness to travel beyond the boundaries of their familiar world into
unknown territory. They used all their senses and wits to read the stars,
winds, seas and landscapes.

Many exercises in this course invite you to become an explorer
of 'inner landscapes' without a clear map of what you are going to
find. Even if your inner landscapes seem familiar and you think you
have already 'mapped them out', we invite you to have another look.
Some of your maps may be outdated. Just as outer landscapes change
with the seasons and weather conditions, inner landscapes change as
well, depending on your bodily, emotional and mental states. What
is there to discover right now? Some inner landscapes may be attractive and welcoming, others barren and forbidding, just as there are
flower meadows and forests as well as deserts and frozen wastes in the
outside world. However, as botanists, wildlife experts and ecologists
know, all landscapes may disclose hidden treasures, no matter how
inhospitable they seem.

Some exercises from the first chapter of this book perhaps raise expectations of pleasant landscapes. These expectations may come true
but you can also make unpleasant discoveries. In this course, we invite
you to be courageous and explore some inner landscapes that seem unattractive at first glance. You may be surprised what there is to discover.

Trust your experience, not your expectations, biases or pre-drawn maps. Have you ever seen those medieval maps with ghastly monsters drawn at the edges of the known world? They did not stop brave discoverers from stepping into the unknown. No doubt they encountered many surprises but certainly not these monsters, which were just figments of the imagination of those first mapmakers. Likewise, you may fear all kinds of demons and dragons when you travel into unknown inner territory. But it may not be as bad as your imagination makes out. What you thought of as your demons may even turn out to be friends awakening compassion in your heart. For the following exercise we were inspired by Tara Brach.[2]

※ COMPASSIONATELY RELATING TO RESISTANCE

Find a comfortable sitting position, being aware of whatever experience arises and letting a soothing breathing rhythm emerge ... (It is good to know that we can start every exercise in this course with these first two steps of the Breathing Space with Kindness, as described on p. 10.)

Then allow a situation to come up, preferably something you recently experienced, which caused a sense of fear, aversion or resistance. You do not have to choose the most difficult situation; just choose something that has been troublesome but you also feel space to work with right now. It can be around a physical or emotional difficulty, or around a difficulty in relating to another person.

If you found something, then allow your imagination to reconnect with the situation and let it come alive as if you are experiencing this difficulty right now. What is there to see, hear, feel... Explore the inner landscape of this sense of threat and your reaction to it. What bodily sensations, what emotions, what thoughts arise...? Allow yourself to be surprised by the details of this landscape. Look around like an explorer would, discovering unknown territory.

Then we invite you to do an experiment and mindfully explore its effects. You are asked to meet the situation and your experience of it with the attitude of 'No, I don't want this'. And really embody this 'No'. Whatever you encounter, meet it with the energy of resistance. 'No' to the situation, 'No' to physical sensations, to emotions, to thoughts, 'No, no, no', embodying the attitude of not-wanting whatever shows up... Even if you have difficulty connecting with the situation or feel reactions against the exercise itself, you can respond with 'No, I don't want this'. 'No' to whatever sound, thought or feeling that shows itself right now. Even 'No' to the breath.

And what effect does this 'No' have on you? What effect does 'No' have on the body, its felt state, its temperature... What are you noticing in your face, jaws, throat, chest, belly, the muscles of your arms and legs, hands and feet? What effect does 'No' have on your mood-state and on your mind? What does it do to the imagined situation? And what would it be like if you maintained this state of 'No' for a much longer period?

Then, let go of 'No' and allow a shift towards a neutral attitude, readjusting your position. If you like, you can open your eyes for a while, take a few deep breaths, and allow the body to move and relax.

continued

Then connect again with this same difficult situation as before, allowing it to come alive in your imagination once more. Allow the landscape to reveal itself again in every detail, bodily, emotionally, mentally... But now experiment with another attitude to meet the situation and your experience of it: the attitude of 'Yes', 'I welcome this' or 'It is okay'. Embody this 'Yes' with your whole being, meeting every experience with a 'Yes', 'Welcome', or 'Okay'. 'Yes' to the situation, to images, emotions, physical sensations... And when the situation itself is not so vivid you can let a 'Yes' flow to whatever you encounter right now. 'Yes' to sounds, thoughts, feelings, 'Yes' to the breath...

While embodying 'Yes', explore what effect it has on you. What effects do you notice in your body, your face, chest, belly, the various muscles in your limbs? What effect does 'Yes' have on your state of mind and your emotional state? What does it do to the imagined situation and your experience of it? And what would it be like if you maintained this 'Yes' for a much longer period?

Then, allow yourself to return to a neutral attitude, in open awareness, allowing the breath to flow freely with whatever arises. You may wish to reflect on the following question: What would be the most compassionate and wise attitude in this given situation, the 'No' or the 'Yes' or perhaps something in between?

This experiment is meant to be an open exploration of possible attitudes, a mindful investigation. There is no underlying judgment that one is better than the other. It may well depend on the situation you have chosen, what the most compassionate response would be. And there may be more than one level to explore: 'Yes' or 'No' to the situation, to your experience of the situation, or to what the exercise brought up. There may also be a difference between 'Yes' and 'Okay' or there may be different types of 'No', like a fearful resisting 'No' or a wise limit-setting 'No'. Gently reflect on whatever arises and you may wish to end by allowing a kind wish to flow through you, on the rhythm of the breath or independently of it.

Questions for reflection

- What situation did you choose?
- What did you notice embodying 'No'?
- What would it be like to persist with 'No' in this situation?
- What did you notice embodying 'Yes' or 'Okay'?
- What would it be like to persist with 'Yes' in this situation?
- Are there any aspects to the situation where 'No' would be more fitting or 'Yes' would be more fitting? For instance, saying 'No' to offensive behaviour from another person, while saying 'Yes' to your feelings.
- What could be a kind wish to yourself or others regarding the theme you have explored?

Outer and inner threats

As we have already seen, from the point of view of evolution, it is crucial for our survival that we are warned against threat. It is no wonder the threat system is the most fundamental and it easily dominates other systems. If we go for a pleasure walk but unexpectedly trip over, we auto-matically stretch out our arms to protect ourselves. If we are enjoying a meal and suddenly we hear the piercing sound of a fire alarm, we forget about the food. The amygdala is a structure in our old brain that oper-ates as an internal alarm bell in response to signals of potential threat. It immediately puts our body in a state of alertness through a cascade of neurobiological and hormonal effects.

Our alarm system becomes more sensitive if we have experienced a lot of threats in our past. As we have already seen, this system has a neg-ativity bias. While the alarm system can be quite effective in protecting us from external threats such as falling on our face or being caught in fire, it can work against us when it responds just as forcefully to inter-nal threats, such as alarming thoughts, painful emotions, or fantasies of doom and gloom. Psychological threats can trigger the same bodily reac-tions as physical threats; the body will not distinguish between the two. This evolutionary mismatch between our old and new brains can cause a lot of suffering. None of this is our fault, it is just how our brains are wired.

Christopher Germer pointed out how the instinctive old brain threat reactions of fight, flight and freeze, which were designed to protect us from external threats, have their psychological new brain equivalents when we feel threatened from inside.[3] Fight takes the form of *self-criticism* or aggression against ourselves. Flight manifests itself as *self-isolation*, in which we hide ourselves from others, feeling alone in our suffering. Freeze takes the form of *over-identification*, where we psychologically freeze into rigid views or 'maps' of ourselves, others and the world around us. These psychological threat reactions may actually have some immediate ad-vantages. Self-criticism, for example, may prevent us being criticised by others, while self-isolation may prevent us being rejected by others and over-identification may protect us against losing control and being ex-posed to unfamiliar views. So, these mechanisms may help us survive psy-chologically, but they cause a lot of suffering in the long run. Fight–flight–freeze reactions may effectively deal with threats from outside. Threats from inside tend to hang around, however. Particularly when we stick to fight-flight-freeze strategies, they may even grow and keep haunting us, like inner demons. Can we respond to inner 'threats' such as emotional pain and upsetting thoughts in healthier ways? Can we meet our inner demons with another attitude than fight–flight–freeze? Yes, indeed we can … with self-compassion.

Three components of self-compassion

Kristin Neff,[4] a pioneering researcher in this field, distinguished three components of self-compassion that offer a remedy against the psycho-logical fight, flight or freeze reactions (see *Figure 2.1*):

- *Self-kindness*, or the capacity to treat ourselves kindly, is the remedy against self-criticism.

- *Common humanity* is the remedy against self-isolation. It is the simple realisation that suffering is part of the human condition and that we share this suffering with many others.
- *Mindfulness* is the remedy against over-identification, or 'frozen' beliefs about our pain and how we should deal with it. Rather than being restricted by narrow perspectives, we mindfully explore our suffering and we respond consciously to it with a non-judgmental mind. Simply holding what we experience in open kind awareness can melt our frozen views.

Figure 2.1 Reactions to threat and self-compassion

You can do a simple but powerful practice we learned from Kristin Neff.[5] It has been referred to as the Self-Compassion Mantra or Self-Compassion Break, which you can do any time you suffer emotional pain. It can ease emotional suffering if you remind yourself regularly of the three aspects of self-compassion, by simply repeating three supportive sentences and letting them resonate in your body and mind. You can put your hand on your heart if you wish.

※ SELF-COMPASSION MANTRA

1 *This is a moment of suffering.*
    (Mindfully acknowledging the suffering – pain, distress, grief, et cetera.)

2 *Suffering is part of being human.*
    (Acknowledging the common humanity of this suffering.)

3 *So may I be kind to myself.*
    (Expressing kindness to the sufferer – yourself.)

Experiment with your own variations of these phrases, finding a version you connect well with. Allow all three components of self-compassion to be voiced. Of course, you may proceed with being kind to yourself in deeds as well.

Another informal practice for times when you encounter a difficulty in your daily life, is an adaptation of the 'coping' version of the Three Minute Breathing Space.[6] You have already learned Breathing Space with Kindness, the 'standard' version, which you can practise any time, planned or unplanned. When kindness meets suffering it becomes compassion. This is why we call this coping exercise Breathing Space with Compassion.

※ BREATHING SPACE WITH COMPASSION

You can do this exercise when experiencing suffering, whenever you are challenged to deal with emotional pain or a stressful situation and it is safe enough to allow for a mindful pause. You can do it while you are sitting, standing or lying down. You can vary the duration, depending on the situation you are in. Again, we distinguish three phases.

1 Being present with open, kind awareness

Acknowledge everything that shows itself, including what feels painful. Notice the sensations as they present themselves. It may be helpful to name them. For instance, 'Tension in my jaw … in my neck … my shoulders', 'Heaviness in my chest', 'Shallow breathing'. Note and name your feelings, e.g. 'Fear', 'Sadness', 'Irritation', 'Shame', 'Vulnerability'. Also, note your thoughts, without losing yourself in their content, e.g. 'Worrying', 'Self-judgment', 'Criticism'. Holding the difficult in a cradle of kindness... Embodying an attitude of soften, sooth, allow … softening bodily tension … soothing painful emotions … allowing thoughts, whatever their content, to come and go...

2 Allowing a soothing breathing rhythm

Observe the movements of the breath and gently allow the breath to slow down and deepen into a calming, comforting rhythm. Let the breath flow freely, allowing the body to soften, gravitating towards the ground that carries you … Perhaps supported by an inner smile, by placing one or both hands on your heart or another gentle touch. Or by connecting with the image of a safe place or a caring other.

3 Letting a compassionate wish flow through the body

Expand your awareness to your entire body, and open your heart for any pain and suffering that may be there right now, whether physically, emotionally or mentally. Ask yourself: What could be a compassionate wish for myself in this moment? And if a wish comes up, softly repeat the words and let the wish flow through you, on the rhythm of the breath, or independent from it. For instance, 'May I feel calm', 'May I feel safe', 'May I receive comfort', 'May I have the courage to be with this pain' 'May I be free from suffering' or 'May I accept what I cannot change'. A paradoxical wish like 'May I feel this tension … this fatigue … this sadness' can be very compassionate, allowing space for what is actually there. The three sentences of the Self-Compassion Mantra may also connect well. Then, resume your daily activities when you are ready to do so.

Tend and befriend

More recently a fourth reaction to threat called 'tend and befriend' has been described in mammalian species.[7] When animals who live in groups sense acute danger, they instinctively care for their young and vulnerable group members ('tend') and seek connection with each other for support ('befriend'). Also, in humans this in-built reaction, designed to help our species survive, can be very strong. It can help survive, but it can also be triggered at the wrong moments. On an aircraft we are specifically warned by safety instructions to put on our own oxygen masks first, before attending to our children. We are urged not to follow our instinct blindly, but use our new brain capacity to put this old brain reaction on hold. On the other hand, our new brains can cause trouble by unnecessarily arousing tend-and-befriend reactions, when we simply imagine others being in danger or in need where they are not. Parents may excessively worry when their toddlers do not finish their plates, although they are thriving well. Or they may spend hours awake, worrying about the safety of their teenagers while they are happily going out with friends.

So tend-and-befriend reactions can – just like fight–flight–freeze reactions – work for us and against us. Many of us have a strong tendency to please others, arising from feeling insecure and a need to be liked. We easily feel compelled to tend to others' needs – real or imagined – at the expense of our own. This can lead to us giving the wrong kind of help to others and forgetting to help ourselves. This may be one explanation for why so many professional and non-professional carers suffer from exhaustion and burn out.

Me-first, you-first or we-together

When we interview people interested in participating in the MBCL courses, many say being compassionate towards others is wearing them out and they would not know how to fit in self-compassion. Later, they begin to discover there is a difference between compassion and being caught in instinctive tend-and-befriend reactions. The new-brain disguises of tend and befriend are self-sacrifice and overanxiety for the welfare of others. While fight–flight–freeze is about the survival of oneself – 'me-first' – tend and befriend is directed at the survival of the other – 'you-first' – or survival of the group. Instinctual reactions are not the same as compassion, however. Tend and befriend is an automatic reaction that – like other stress reactions – can be helpful in case of acute external threat but it drains energy if it persists any longer than necessary. It is part of our design, which is not our fault, but the challenge is to deal with it wisely. When we allow ourselves to pause in awareness and move from threat to soothing system, we can step out of automatic reactions and choose a conscious compassionate response, considering the needs of all involved. This has the quality of 'we-together', instead of me-first or you-first.

Survival of the kindest

Biologist Frans de Waal,[8] argues that the general use of the phrase 'survival of the fittest' has little to do with Darwin's original idea of evolution by natural selection. Darwin himself was disappointed that his theory was often misinterpreted by those in power, and misused by the rich to exploit the poor. The original meaning of the term 'fittest' is not 'strongest', but 'the best adapted to the environment'. So, 'survival of the fittest' is no excuse for indulging in primitive reptilian brain desires, as if evolution had stopped there. When the mammalian brain enabled animals to cooperate, share and care for each other it was a quantum leap in evolution. And like no other animal, humans are extremely vulnerable and dependent on care for many years into adulthood. Our capacity for empathy and morality and for cooperative and altruistic behaviour increases survival chances. Some psychologists proposed we should replace 'survival of the fittest' with 'survival of the nurtured'[9] or 'survival of the kindest'.[10] It is not being strong but being kind and caring that gives the best survival chances for the human species. A participant in one of our workshops who was a keen motorcyclist thought the text *Born to be wild* on his T-shirt should be replaced with *Born to be mild.*

Nowadays, evolution scientists and religious leaders do not oppose each other as much as they did in the previous century. Evolutionists increasingly acknowledge the survival value of religions. Religious leaders, like the Dalai Lama, speak about kindness and compassion as basic needs for humanity, which can be cultivated independently from religion. Surely, religion *can* contribute to a kinder world, although this may not always be obvious from the behaviour of its followers. Nevertheless, Karen Armstrong, a historian in comparative religious studies, found compassion to be the core value of all major religions and wisdom traditions.[11]

Now, let us return to the cultivation of kindness towards ourselves and say a bit more about the practice of self-compassion.

Pathways to self-compassion

In old Asian languages, the word for compassion is *karuna*, referring to *all* beings, including ourselves. In Western cultures, the word 'self-compassion' had to be created. We seem to have forgotten the second half of the biblical message to love your neighbour *as yourself.* Is it because our mind is narrowed by a 'you-first' focus (tend and befriend) or because of our culture-based fears of self-pity and indulgence? Whatever may be the reason for this imbalance, self-pity narrows the mind around ourselves as the suffering centre of the world, whereas self-compassion opens the mind towards suffering as part of the human condition. A genuinely compassionate attitude towards our own suffering is not selfish but increases our sensitivity to all suffering, no matter who is doing the suffering. So, although we distinguish compassion towards others and self-compassion, it is important to remember that they are inseparable.

Christopher Germer[12] helpfully described five pathways to practising self-compassion, which are presented in the overview below.

The way of ...	Characterised by ...	Practice
1 The body	Softening	Physical rest and relaxation, offering the body warmth, support and gentle exercise (bath, sauna, body scan, yoga, dance, sports, pleasure walk). Nourishing the body through all senses such as visual beauty, comforting sound, touch, fragrance, taste.
2 Emotions	Soothing	Befriending these inner messengers, even if they feel unpleasant. Holding painful emotions in the kind embrace of awareness, like a caring mother holds her upset child.
3 Thoughts	Allowing	An open, non-judgmental attitude towards thoughts and mental images, simply acknowledging their coming and going while not having to control, escape or follow them.
4 Relations	Intimacy, connectedness, generosity	Treating others as you wish to be treated yourself (The Golden Rule). Sharing ups and downs with sensitivity to each other's needs. Nurturing 'we-together' instead of 'me-first' or 'you-first'.
5 Spirituality	Commitment to deeper, non-selfish values	Setting and re-setting your intentions to connect to what you really value. Listening to what touches your heart and gives your life meaning.

What all these pathways of self-compassion have in common is that they open 'the heart'. Here, we do not mean the organ that pumps blood around, but the felt sense of the heart. This central area in our chest sensitively informs us about the quality of connection with whatever shows up in our awareness, whether physical sensations, emotions, thoughts, other beings or meaningful values. The heart closes when we are stressed and try to keep out what we do not want or hold on to what we want. The heart opens when we relax and positively resonate with life as it unfolds. Hand in hand with mindfulness, we can practise 'heartfulness', by exploring the pathways that open our heart. A very simple practice is to place a hand on your heart. If you like, you can try it now.

※ A HAND ON YOUR HEART

Allow for a mindful pause ... the eyes may be open or closed ... acknowledging your position and whatever is there to notice right now, in the surroundings and in the body, whether sounds, feelings, thoughts ... letting the breath find its soothing rhythm...

> *Remind yourself of an experience that touched your heart and gave you feelings of joy, peace, contentment ... perhaps you were on your own or sharing this experience with a beloved person, or a pet... Allow a smile to appear as you remember it...*
>
> *Imagine you are softly breathing through your heart and letting it become spacious... Now, gently place an open hand on the region of your heart ... feeling the touch and warmth... How is it received? ... feel the sensations in your hand, in your chest, on the surface and inside... Which effects do you notice in the body and the mind? What effect does it have on your mood? Acknowledge your experience, just as it is.*

We regularly invite you to place one or both hands on your heart during exercises. You may find it strange at first. Quite likely it will become more familiar when you practise this heart-awareness, which you can do any time, noticing whether it feels open or closed, spacious or tight, warm or cold, light or heavy. And if the heart feels closed, explore what it needs to open. That might be the touch of your hand, a soothing breath, a kind word or a comforting image. Also, when you do your formal meditation practices, it can be helpful to place a hand on your heart now and then.

When compassion itself seems to be the demon

Perhaps everything that frightens us
is in its deepest essence
something helpless that wants our help.
—Rainer Maria Rilke[13]

Quite often, kindness and compassion themselves give rise to threat reactions. As if inner demons do indeed pop up from the unknown. The challenge is not to slip back into fight–flight–freeze mode but to offer them understanding and care. If self-criticism has become a habit – your 'comfort zone' – and you begin to explore the rather unknown territory of self-kindness, it is understandable that you will encounter fear. This will happen all the more if self-kindness uncovers old hurts and unfulfilled needs. Paul Gilbert acknowledges the fear of compassion as an important theme in therapy.[14] Christopher Germer uses the term 'backdraft' for adverse reactions to self-compassion in general.[15] We like to work with different metaphors to explain what can happen.

Fear, anger, mistrust

Imagine a stray dog roaming the streets in a country where most dogs are treated badly. It probably suffered a lot of neglect and abuse during its lifetime. Coming from a culture where people are fond of dogs, you may be tempted to walk up to the poor animal and stroke it. But the dog will not appreciate this kindness if it is not familiar with it. Instead, it will be on guard, growling at you in defence, ready to attack or run off. Forcing kindness upon this dog would only make matters worse. It first needs to learn you can be trusted before it can receive a tiny bit of kindness from you. This requires patience and a gentle approach. Instead of walking up to the dog it is better to wait until the dog is ready to come to you. Likewise, forcing kindness on neglected parts in yourself can cause fear, anger and mistrust.

Panic

'Backdraft' is a term used by firemen for one of the dangers of entering a burning building. In an enclosed compartment, where there is heat but no flames because the oxygen ran out, a sudden air-stream from a broken window or an opened door can cause an explosion of fire. Similarly, a sudden panic can occur when kindness enters an area that has been depleted from it. This can happen when kindness is linked to traumatic experiences, such as being abused or deserted by someone who first treated you kindly. You may have learned to seal yourself off from kindness to make sure a bad experience does not repeat itself. As we said, the body reacts the same to real and imagined threats. To *know* this can already help, but it also needs mindful practice for the body to *feel* that false alarms can be calmed by your soothing system.

Grief

Whereas backdraft is a 'hot' metaphor, here is a 'cold' metaphor, that may be more fitting for the experience of grief. If you ever played in the snow as a child, making snowballs with bare hands, you might remember how much it hurt when you tried to warm your almost frozen fingers near a heater or under a hot-water tap. Your fingers needed the warmth to stay alive, but the kindest way was to administer it slowly, holding them under a cold-water tap, then slightly warmer, and warmer again. Just as effective, but with much less pain. Similarly, if your need for love and warmth was not met when you were young, you may have learned to deny this need. If a wave of warmth enters these 'frozen' areas they can react with pangs of grief, feeling the pain of what you missed then, and perhaps all those years until now. The kindest way to let the warmth flow back into these areas, is to do it slowly.

A gentle pace

Adverse reactions to kindness and compassion are common in people who were neglected, abandoned or maltreated as children. Those who were not securely bonded to their parents or caregivers often find it difficult to trust others and form stable relationships later in life.[16] Their relationships do not provide a secure base to explore the world from, or a safe haven to return to when the seas outside are rough. Insecure attachment is by no means rare. But even if you were securely attached, there may be areas of unmet needs in your life, causing you some trouble when those areas are finally seen and approached kindly. Many people experience adverse reactions in more subtle ways, as tenderness, sadness, heaviness or emptiness. You may notice this more clearly when you observe yourself mindfully.

The important message is that adverse reactions to receiving kindness are a normal phenomenon that many of us will encounter. Adverse reactions are not 'wrong' reactions, they arise naturally from our histories. So, if you notice them, there is nothing wrong with you. It is another opportunity to practise mindfulness and awaken compassion. Having a grounding in mindfulness practice is particularly helpful here, enabling you to pause with your experience as it is, even if it is painful and difficult, allowing the breath to settle into a soothing rhythm and the body to soften. Ask yourself: What would a compassionate response be right now? It might be a kind word, phrase or gesture, like a hand on the heart or an inner smile towards the difficulty that has arisen. And if an exercise is overwhelming, you may always stop and return to it when you feel more space. Be compassionate to yourself by adjusting the dose of kindness and administering it at a gentle pace. Even then, it may still hurt. It is a healing pain, however. A part in you that was not being seen and cared for is now reconnected to the stream of life.

Wobbles on the way

In the previous paragraphs we discussed a few difficulties in the practice. We do not wish to discourage you, but there are many more. The good news is that they are not evidence of failure but *part of the practice*. All obstacles are a kind of suffering and can help to awaken compassion in ourselves. In fact, it would be more difficult to develop compassion if everything went smoothly. Below, we list some common obstacles people encounter and offer examples of compassionate responses.

Difficulties with motivation	Compassionate response
Lack of motivation, not finding time to practise, losing interest.	Acknowledging the doubt or disconnection with the practice. Reflecting on your deeper motivations and values, and why you would wish to cultivate kindness and compassion (see questions in the introduction); re-setting your intentions.
Forceful discipline, a strong sense of duty or striving for results.	Recognising threat or drive motivations creeping into your practice (predominant verbs: 'should', 'ought', 'must', 'want'). Allowing space for the soothing system and a playful attitude (predominant verbs: 'allow', 'may', 'wish', 'grant').

continued

Difficulties with motivation	Compassionate response
Difficulty in choosing what to practise or feeling overwhelmed by too many exercises.	Noticing the doubt and asking yourself what you need right now. Is it in line with what you really value? Which exercises do you connect well with and would be kind to practise and deepen in the week that lies ahead?

Unhelpful expectations	Compassionate response
'My pain will go away.'	The practice is not about making unpleasant feelings go away but about relating to them in a compassionate way. Always start where you are. Experiment with paradoxical wishes such as 'May I feel this pain/ resistance/ restlessness/ irritation' or 'May I experience this just as it is'.
'My wishes (e.g. for health or happiness) will come true.'	Recognising unhelpful attachments to outcome. The practice is about cultivating an inner attitude of kindness rather than striving for results. It is more about goodwill than about getting good feelings. You may trust that practice fertilises the ground in which positive feelings can grow. You cannot force them to grow; they will come in their own time. This is more likely if you don't strive.
'Adverse reactions will not occur.'	Painful reactions are part of the practice. 'Backdraft' is normal and asks for a gentle pace.

Unhelpful beliefs	Compassionate response
'Self-compassion is self-indulgent.'	When you practise self-compassion, you develop a sensitivity to pain and suffering, whoever is the sufferer. Self-pity is self-centred, but self-compassion opens the mind to common humanity.
'Compassion is for softies. It will make me weak and lazy.'	The practice is not about glossing over reality with a sugar coating but facing experience as it is, including the difficult. It requires courage, strength and perseverance to face the difficult and do what is needed to ease suffering.
'Self-criticism keeps me sharp and prevents me from making mistakes.'	Kindness is a better teacher than fear. Fear of making mistakes will keep you in your comfort zone. Kindness will invite you to explore new possibilities and learn from mistakes.
'Practising with these wishes and phrases is like brainwashing.'	Neurons that fire together, wire together. So, why not put repetition to work at the service of your well-being? Science confirms that kindness and compassion are to the brain what the breath is to life.[17]
'Imagery is not real, so there is no point in putting a lot of effort into this kind of practice.'	Imagery is indeed not the same as real life. However, imagery has real effects, both pleasant and unpleasant. So, it is wise to put your effort into imagery with wholesome effects.
'As it deals with suffering, compassion practice should always be done in earnest.'	Not at all! Humour, playfulness, appreciative joy, smiling at life's imperfections are all part of the practice. It's a challenge to welcome wobbles on the way and not take them personally.

Using imagery

... knowledge is limited, whereas imagination encircles the world.
—Albert Einstein[18]

As we do a lot of imagery work in compassion training, it may be helpful to say a bit more about how imagery works. Do you ever lie awake at night, imagining what could go wrong the next day, fearing a whole range of doom scenarios? Or were you, as a child, ever unable to fall asleep because thinking about Christmas presents kept you in a state of ongoing excitement? Such images, although they are not 'real', have real effects on our body and mind to such an extent that they keep us awake. Just like our old-brain threat and drive systems easily overrule the soothing system, our new-brain imagination often automatically focusses on what we fear or desire, rather than what calms and comforts us. Often, the default mode of our imagination adds to our stress levels. We need mindfulness to step out of this and allow the mind to create images that soothe us.

Here are some examples of how imagination affects us. If you are enjoying a nice meal, various bodily changes occur, such as production of saliva and gastric juices. This will happen as soon as you first smell the food or take a first bite. Now, when you are hungry and you just imagine your favourite dish in front of your nose, you will quite likely have the same response. Similarly, when you engage in enjoyable sexual activity, you experience physical arousal and desire. But when you only imagine making love, your body shows the same reactions. Our old brains and bodies do not appear to know the difference between a real and an imagined stimulus. This can work for and against us.

In situations in which you are being shamed or bullied, you experience intense bodily and emotional stress reactions. Just imagining being shamed or criticised can result in similar stress reactions. And if this becomes a habit, you may become increasingly anxious, irritable or depressed. On the other hand, if you find yourself in a kind and caring environment you feel comfortable, contented and relaxed. The same reactions may also happen when just imagining it. This usually requires a bit more practice than in the first three examples, where imagery often operates on autopilot.

Modern neuroscience confirms that practice changes our brains. The brain's capacity to change with experience is called 'neuroplasticity'.[19] In this process, neurons form new networks. With mindfulness and compassion training, we can train the brain to work for us. When we nourish the soothing system, and train ourselves using imagery with wholesome effects, we can re-wire our brains. So, here is another imagery practice for you to try out.

※ A COMPASSIONATE COMPANION

You can start with step one and two of The Breathing Space with Kindness, mindfully holding in your awareness what presents itself in this moment ... allowing a soothing breathing rhythm... And any time you can return to these two steps.

continued

Do not force anything in this exercise, allow a playful atmosphere. Let yourself be surprised by the free gift of your imagination. You can start with the image of a safe place, in whatever way it presents itself now ... allowing all senses to be involved ... a place welcoming you, however you feel in the present moment ... Then allow another image to emerge from this safe place or independently from it, opening yourself for the presence of a compassionate being that has your best interests at heart... It can arise from memory or fantasy or both. It can be a human being, or an animal, a natural being, or a celestial being... In any case a being that is committed to your well-being, embodying compassion in all its qualities ... it is kind and patient, sensitive, playful and caring, wise and understanding; it has courage and resilience in the face of life's difficulties, staying firmly on your side when you suffer, accepting you just as you are, with all your imperfections and possibilities, wishing you the very best from its heart, and willing to relieve your suffering wherever it can.

What does your compassionate companion look like? What colour, what shape ... big or small ... old or young ... male or female ... where in space is it positioned ... in front of you, beside or behind you ... at what distance? The visual image may vary in clarity, various images may come and go ... If this compassionate friend looked at you, how would you imagine the expression of the eyes and the face... Other senses may be clearer ... perhaps a feeling sense of presence or atmosphere, perhaps a fragrance... How would this being relate to you? If it spoke to you, how would the voice sound?

What effect does imagining yourself being near this compassionate being have on you? What bodily effects do you notice ... in your face, your chest, your belly, your arms and legs? ... What happens to your thoughts and feelings, your mind, your mood state? ... Just imagine this being really appreciating your presence and your company. No matter how you are, it welcomes you from the heart... How does that make you feel?

And remember, it is a practice. It may be difficult to connect to it, or various fleeting images may pass by. Notice your reactivity to what arises, your likes and dislikes. Acknowledge and welcome whatever shows itself, pleasant or unpleasant, joyful or sad, tendencies to hold on or hold off... Any moment allow for a mindful pause ... allowing the breath to soothe you ... and when you feel the space, return to the imagery practice ... imagining a compassionate being relating to you with this very experience you have right now. The following lines may offer inspiration:

> Don't walk in front of me. I may not follow
> Don't walk behind me. I may not lead.
> Just walk beside me and be my friend.
> —Anonymous

You can continue for a while with this practice of imagining a compassionate friend. When you are ready to end it, allow time for expressing appreciation or a goodbye, in your own way, and let the image dissolve. You can return any moment to this practice of imagining a compassionate being, wherever you are, and however it shows itself.

Questions for reflection

- What being(s) appeared during the exercise?
- Which sense qualities were most clearly present (seeing, hearing, smelling, feeling)?
- Which physical sensations, thoughts and feelings did you notice?

- What was it like to imagine that the compassionate being really appreciated you?
- What are you noticing now, while reflecting on the exercise?
- What could be a kind wish now?

If you wish, you can continue with the Kindness Meditation towards yourself this week or you can expand the practice towards somebody else. Traditionally, the next phase in the practice is sending kindness to a benefactor.

※ KINDNESS MEDITATION: A BENEFACTOR

First practise Kindness Meditation towards yourself as described on p. 20.

Then, expand the practice to another person. Let somebody arise in your mind whom you consider to be a benefactor, an example of wisdom and compassion, alive or deceased... It can be a dear relative, a teacher, an inspiring historical, religious or political figure ... somebody radiating goodness into the world... It may be helpful to imagine this person in front of you at a comfortable distance and looking into his or her eyes and face... How does this affect you?... Then gently begin repeating wishes of kindness towards this person, if you like, on the soothing rhythm of the breath. For instance, on the in-breath 'May you...' and on the out-breath '... feel safe ... healthy ... happy ... at ease' or any other wish that comes from you heart and connects with this person... Gently repeat this wish and mindfully observe the effect of this practice on your body, your thoughts and feelings...

If difficult emotions arise – you may, for instance, feel sad because you miss the actual presence of this benefactor or worry about his or her welfare – then do not hesitate to allow a mindful pause ... allowing the breath to return to a soothing rhythm and letting a kind or compassionate wish flow towards yourself... When you feel the space to return, resume your kind wishes towards this person... 'May you ... be free from suffering ... be joyful ... be in peace...' and so on.

You may wish to expand the practice to other benefactors and continue for a little longer... Then, end the practice in your own time.

※ Calendar: Threat System

This week, specifically notice moments during which the threat system is spontaneously activated in daily life. See if you can mindfully explore these threat reactions, asking yourself what a compassionate response could be. You can note down your experiences on Worksheet 8.

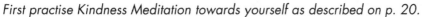

Questions for reflection

- What was the situation?
- How and when did you become aware of the threat system?
- Which physical sensations did you notice?

continued

- Which thoughts and emotions did you notice?
- What are you noticing now while reflecting on this experience?
- What could be a compassionate response?

SUMMARY CHAPTER 2

In this chapter we pay attention to stress reactions in the face of threat, like fight–flight–freeze and tend-and-befriend. We show how similar reactions occur with physical and psychological threat. We explore the pathways to self-compassion and how we can work with imagery. We explain how adverse reactions to compassion itself can arise and how to deal with backdraft and other obstacles in the practice.

SUGGESTIONS FOR PRACTICE

Formal

- Explore Compassionately Relating to Resistance. 🔊 📝
- Regularly practise a Compassionate Companion. 🔊 📝
- Continue with the practices from Chapter 1 that connect well with you and you can expand the Kindness Meditation with the benefactor. 🔊

Informal

- Regularly practise the Breathing Space with Kindness and when you encounter difficulty and painful emotions you can practise the Breathing Space with Compassion 🔊 or the Self-Compassion Mantra (p. 30).
- Explore the Hand on Your Heart exercise (p. 34).
- Calendar: Threat System. 📝

Notes

1. Freely translated from Proust, M. (1925). *À la recherche du temps perdu – La Prisonnière, éd. Gallimard*, p. 69.
2. Brach, T. (2004). *Radical acceptance: Embracing your life with the heart of a Buddha*. New York: Bantam.
3. Germer, C. K. (2009). *The mindful path to self-compassion*. New York: Guilford Press.
4. Neff, K. D. (2003). Self-compassion: An alternative conceptualization of a healthy attitude toward oneself. *Self and Identity, 2*, 85–102.
5. Neff, K. (2011). *Self-compassion: Stop beating yourself up and leave insecurity behind*. New York: HarperCollins.
6. Segal, S. V., Williams, J. M. G., & Teasdale, J. D. (2013). *Mindfulness-based cognitive therapy for depression*. New York: Guilford Press.

7. Taylor, S. (2006). Tend and befriend: Biobehavioral bases of affiliation under stress. *Current Directions in Psychological Science, 15,* 273–277.

8. De Waal, F. (2009). *The age of empathy: Nature's lessons for a kinder society.* New York: Three Rivers Press.

9. Cozolino, L. (2006). *The neuroscience of human relationships: Attachment and the developing social brain.* New York: Norton.

10. Keltner, D. (2009). *Born to be good: The science of a meaningful life.* New York: Norton.

11. Armstrong, K. (2011). *Twelve steps to a compassionate life.* London: The Bodley Head.

12. Germer, C. K. (2009). *The mindful path to self-compassion.* New York: Guilford Press.

13. Freely translated from Rilke, R.M. (1929). *Briefe an einen jungen Dichter.* Insel Verlag, p. 48.

14. Gilbert, P. (2010). *Compassion focused therapy.* London: Routledge.

15. Germer, C. K. (2009). *The mindful path to self-compassion.* New York: Guilford Press.

16. Mikulincer, M. & Shaver, P.R. (2007). *Attachment in adulthood: Structure, dynamics and change.* New York: Guilford Press.

17. Siegel, D. J. (2010). *The mindful therapist: A clinician's guide to mindsight and neural integration.* New York: W.W. Norton.

18. Albert Einstein quoted in 'What life means to Einstein: An interview by George Sylvester Viereck' in *The Saturday Evening Post* (26 October 1929).

19. Davidson, R. J. (2012). The neurobiology of compassion. In C. K. Germer & R. D. Siegel (eds), *Compassion and wisdom in psychotherapy* (pp. 111–118). New York, NY: Guilford Press.

Chapter 3

Treating habits kindly

Session three: untangling desires and patterns

This is the very perfection of man, to find out his own imperfections.

—St Augustine of Hippo

In the previous chapter you were invited to explore quite different inner landscapes. Landscapes shaped by external or internal threats, and landscapes of soothing images, such as a safe place or a compassionate companion. You may have noticed how changeable the landscapes can be, depending on inner weather conditions. In this chapter, we will explore more inner landscapes, beginning with a landscape related to the drive system.

Ulysses' courage

Did you ever hear Homer's story of Ulysses and the Sirens?[1] Sirens were beautiful but dangerous female creatures whose enchanting singing lured sailors to their cliffs. Sailors who could not resist ended up being killed. The Sirens then used the human bones to make their musical instruments. Ulysses took on the challenge to resist the Sirens and ordered his crew to tie him firmly to the mast, so he could not leave the ship. His men protected themselves by putting wax in their ears. Ulysses himself was fully exposed to the haunting singing and the aching desires when he sailed past the Sirens. Nevertheless, he survived and learned that even the strongest desire eventually fades.

Now for the next exercise[2] you need a bit of Ulysses' courage to look into the nature of desire. Unlike Ulysses, we suggest you begin with a desire of modest intensity and explore it mindfully.

※ COMPASSIONATELY RELATING TO DESIRE

Choose a comfortable position, allowing space for step one and two of the Breathing Space with Kindness.

In this exercise, you are invited to explore an area of desire or attachment in your life, which feels rather uncomfortable and can be a source of suffering. Choose an area that feels okay to explore right now. Just in case nothing much shows up, we give a few examples. It may be a desire to eat unhealthy foods, smoke or drink alcohol. It may be a desire to buy things you do not really need, a desire to play games, compulsively check emails, surf the internet or follow social media. It may be a sexual desire or a desire to be seen by others, a need to be right, to be funny or to be admired. Let it be a desire that you experience regularly in your everyday life and you find difficult to resist. Something that easily causes frustration or feelings of shame or guilt when you are in its grip.

If an area has come up, bring it to life by imagining a recent situation where this desire was prominent. Imagine you are feeling the desire right now, as if you are again in that same situation. You can imagine it becoming stronger and stronger... But, even when the object of your desire comes closer and closer, you withstand the temptation to satisfy it...

Now, explore the inner landscape of desire with the curiosity of an explorer being open to every detail of it. How is the desire affecting your body and posture ... what happens in your face, your chest, your belly ... what about the muscles in different parts of the body ... what happens to the state of your mood and your mind?

And while you are observing the nature of desire, just let some questions drop in, not needing to force an answer. Perhaps there is no answer. Perhaps there are several answers. Either is okay. Just let yourself be surprised.

Ask yourself: Is there anything lying underneath this desire? ... Is there perhaps an emotion or a deeper need, hidden under the desire you are exploring?... What is actually going on under the surface?... Is there a deeper longing for something you really value?

Listen with your heart for possible answers, while gently repeating these questions in various forms... If nothing in particular comes up, just continue to explore the nature of desire as it shows itself moment by moment and observe your reactions... Then, probe again what resonates while the question sinks in deeper.

If something comes up, you are invited to respond to it with a kind, compassionate wish. Meeting the deeper needs of yourself as a vulnerable human being, who shares similar needs with many others. Just welcome what comes up... Perhaps a wish for calm and patience, a wish for comfort, understanding or connection, or a wish to simply give space to whatever shows itself... And then gently repeat the wish, if you like on the soothing rhythm of the breath, offering it to yourself and sensing how it is received ... continuing with this as long as you like.

Questions for reflection

- What area of desire or attachment did you explore?
- Which physical sensations, thoughts and feelings did you notice?

continued

- What answer(s) came up with the question 'Is there anything that lies underneath this desire?'
- What did you wish for yourself? How was this received inside?
- What is happening now, while you reflect on the exercise?
- What could be a kind, compassionate wish right now?

Urge-surfing

This exercise is not meant to suggest you should always expect to find something underlying your everyday desires that you need to deal with. One way of compassionately relating to desire can involve simply being present with the desire without giving in to it. Mindfully surfing on the wave as the desire grows, peaks and eventually subsides is called 'urge-surfing'.[3] It may prove worthwhile to explore what is under the surface, as we invite you to do in the exercise. Another way may be kindly giving in to the desire, but then following this process mindfully and noticing what unfolds moment by moment. Often, we either repress or satisfy our desires on autopilot. Bringing mindfulness to the process can make a major difference. We develop more sensitivity in noticing what the nature of desire and satisfaction actually is.

Why we can't get no satisfaction[4]

From an evolutionary point of view the drive system is designed to make sure we grab what we can whenever we can. When our ancestors lived in times of scarcity it was important to have a strong reward system to make us hunt for prey. Developing strong appetites for food and sex greatly increased our chances of survival, as an individual and as a species. Getting what we want gives an immediate but short-lived satisfaction so that we seek to repeat this experience again and again. When scarcity is the rule, it will not harm us to eat as much as we can. It may be a long time before we catch the next meal. Our so-called satiety system, which gives us the message we have had enough, is therefore rather insensitive.[5] There is no need to be judgmental about this, it is simply part of our design and no fault of our own. Tendencies that are useful when supplies are scarce can create problems in times of abundance. Some desires can really make us suffer if we give in to them. In our modern lives, we are surrounded by food. If we follow our desires blindly, we can easily eat too much, which may lead to obesity, heart disease and diabetes. It is an evolutionary mismatch that leads us to consume more than needed. It can also lead to problems in other areas. We can have voracious appetites for all kinds of indulgences and the money that can buy them. The same applies to information and knowledge, admiration and success, 'followers' and 'likes' on social media.

It can alleviate a lot of suffering if we learn to deal with our desires wisely and compassionately. Mindfully surfing the waves of our desires can help us realise, like Ulysses, that even strong desires will fade. Mindfully noticing when desires are fulfilled can help us sense we have had enough.

Habits and patterns

There is a native American story about a wise old Indian who teaches his grandson about life. He says: 'Deep inside me there is an ongoing battle between two wolves. One wolf is evil. It is rage, fear, self-pity, envy, greed, deceit and selfishness. The other wolf is good. It is kindness, joy, love, hope, generosity, honesty and compassion. This is a terrible battle. This same battle is raging in you and in every human being.' The grandson thinks about this for a while and then he asks: 'Which wolf wins?' The old man smiles and simply answers: 'The one you feed.'

This story reminds us that we have a choice in life as to what qualities in ourselves we 'feed' by nourishing them with attention and spending time and energy on them. We develop a lot of habits without conscious choice, however. They help us deal more efficiently with recurring circumstances. Just think how complicated life would be if we had to figure out how to brush our teeth every day or how to drive a car. Doing these tasks on autopilot saves a lot of energy. Habits grow ever stronger by repetition and they become deeply wired into our brains. And the stronger the neural networks become, the more easily habits are repeated. Both old and new brain processes are involved in this.

Inner patterns are persistent habits in the way we think, feel and behave. They are also called mindsets, modes, schemas or scripts and offer us blueprints on how to live in our complex societies. They are a combination of old-brain instincts with new-brain features such as imagery, thinking and reasoning. Our new brains enable us to make mental pictures and tell stories about ourselves, others and the world we live in. They automatically pop up whenever the circumstances trigger them. This is very helpful if the scripts still fit the bill, but they can cause a lot of trouble when they do not. The most salient patterns evolved around interpersonal relating. Some are characteristic of entire cultures and others are more specific for smaller groups, families or individuals. There appear to be patterns that are so universal that they run through most cultures, past and present. They evolve around themes that are important in all societies such as power and submission, authority and obedience, rivalry and rank, cooperating and caring, male and female roles.[6] Even these patterns may change over time, depending on how much they are fed. Patterns we learned from early childhood often operate largely unconsciously. They are so deeply wired that they are difficult to unlearn. Fortunately, the practice of mindfulness can help us become aware of them, so it becomes easier to stop feeding them and respond to what life asks from us right now.

Three basic modes

A helpful model for talking about patterns is to distinguish the six components as shown in the diagrams below. There is a basic *motivation* that stimulates our *imagination*, focusses our *attention*, guides our *reasoning*, directs our *behaviour* and colours our *emotions*. Based on Paul Gilbert's work we give three examples of patterns where the old-brain emotion regulation systems are intertwined with new-brain functions.[7]

Threat mode

If we learn to see the world as a place full of sticks that can harm us, we easily develop a threat mode (*Figure 3.1*). Our primary motivation is to protect ourselves, so we are constantly on our guard and our attention is focussed on signs of danger. Threats may come from outside such as when we feel shamed, blamed or rejected by others or from inside when we meet emotional pain. We create images and stories around what already went wrong and could go wrong again. Our behaviour is avoidant or resistant and emotionally we feel anxious, irritable or suspicious. Being overly sensitive to danger and wary of people is the basis for all our reasoning. You will surely agree that this is not the type of inner landscape you would like to inhabit for long.

Figure 3.1 Threat Mode

The threat mode is sadly the dominant script for many people. The reasons may be obvious, such as living in a war zone or being hit by natural disaster. At least people can support each other during such predicaments, driven by tend and befriend reactions. Sometimes, the reasons for a dominant threat mode are more hidden. Coming from an unstable home background, suffering personal trauma such as sexual or emotional abuse, being bullied at school or exploited at work are just a few examples. In these cases, people may feel much more isolated, sometimes suffering in silence for years. Many exacerbate their own inner landscape of threat by judging themselves harshly. We will look at this in more detail later.

Competition mode

Another common pattern is the competition mode (*Figure 3.2*), which commonly develops when we learn to perceive the world as a place full of desirable carrots. Here, self-improvement and enrichment are the basic motivations. Our attention is drawn towards possible rewards from outside such as being liked and admired, higher rank and status or from inside such as feelings of pleasure and satisfaction. We fantasise about success and fame, we strive and compete for better results and our emotions alternate between craving and excitement as well as frustration and envy. Our reasoning is driven by all these things.

Figure 3.2 Competition Mode

This inner landscape may not feel quite as tense as that of the threat mode, but it is far from calm and peaceful. Although feelings of satisfaction are pleasant they do not last long. In this script, there are always more needs to satisfy and another half-empty glass that needs topping up. The competition mode is continually being fed in our modern Western culture with its emphasis on individuality and the pressure to prove oneself. We strive for better results, more success, more income, more friends, more certificates, more possessions, more, more, more ... including more self-esteem. The seeds may have been planted in our families and fuelled at school. Nowadays, not many school teachers believe that harsh punishments yield better results. Using rewards in education was an improvement on yesterday's teaching methods. But if self-esteem becomes a goal in itself and is dependent on approval of others, it will be difficult to feel at ease, as the threat mode will kick in easily. Children may feel caught between the need to be on top and the fear of losing out. Neither of these is a good recipe for happiness.

Caring mode

Recent research suggests that self-esteem is not the *cause* of better achievements, but the *result*. In fact, self-compassion appears to be more strongly associated with happiness and better achievements than self-esteem.[8] Self-compassion encourages social connection rather than competition as it encourages awareness of common humanity. What if schools and families valued self-compassion rather than self-esteem and created an environment where children learn to cooperate rather than compete? Being less focused on outcome and feeling at ease allows more space for curiosity, creativity and learning. Adults also thrive better in caring environments rather than competitive ones. In the short run, companies that care for their employees and the environment may make less profit, but in the long run they may well be more sustainable, as argued by scholars like Thupten Jinpa,[9] and Matthieu Ricard.[10] So, cultivating compassion rather than competition may even be good for the economy.

Figure 3.3 Caring Mode

Figure 3.3 shows how a caring mode might look. Care for well-being and social connection could be the basic motivation. Our attention would not be focused on sticks or carrots, but be open to both the needs of ourselves and others. A non-judgmental attitude would be the starting point for our reasoning, allowing space for new perspectives and possibilities. We would not be focussed on the past but look positively to the future and we would see the glass as half-full rather than half-empty. Our behaviour would be kind and respectful and our emotions would be characterised by ease, contentment and gratitude.

Love thy inner critic as thyself

Just as we develop patterns in relating to others and the world around us, we also develop patterns in how we deal with ourselves. In the previous chapter, we already described our tendency to be self-critical and turn the negativity bias inward. We often look at ourselves in a judgmental way. We make mental pictures of how we are and how we should be. We compare the two and the wider the gap, the stronger our tendency to criticise ourselves. We may either harshly judge our actual self: 'You're no good', 'You're so stupid' or 'You're just a loser'; or we may push ourselves toward our ideal self: 'You can do better than this', 'You must stand out from the rest' or 'You should make your parents proud'. So, we either stimulate our threat mode or our competition mode, or both. Many people do this persistently, out of habit. An inner critic develops, or even worse an inner bully, who is rarely satisfied and keeps haunting us, harassing us for every minor imperfection.

As it is so common, there must be some advantages in having an inner critic. Participants of MBCL training groups usually have no difficulty identifying these. They say things like:

- I had better criticise myself before others criticise me.
- It prevents me being rejected by others.
- It keeps me from making mistakes.
- It makes me perform better.
- We all do this in our family.

There may be self-protection motives underlying our self-criticism. The inner critic may well have an intention to help us. However, when it gets out of hand and the tone becomes hostile and self-criticism turns into self-loathing and self-hate, the inner critic becomes an inner bully. Just as polluted landscapes in the outer world become increasingly unpleasant to live and breathe in, it is difficult to feel at ease in an inner landscape constantly poisoned by negative comments. Fighting back by criticising our inner critic is just adding more of the same. So, is there a way to befriend our inner critic and clean up this inner pollution?

A first step can be to have some understanding of the underlying emotions that feed the inner critic.

Self-conscious emotions

In the course of evolution, along with developing self-awareness and awareness of how others view us, we developed so-called 'self-conscious emotions'.[11] These are emotions such as shame, guilt, embarrassment, shyness, envy or pride. The inner critic very much feeds on emotions related to negative self-evaluation. Just like other emotions they are neither good nor bad. Although they may feel unpleasant, they may carry important messages that help us fit in with others and secure our position in groups. Here are the most important ones.

Shame

This can be a very powerful feeling. Shame is rather old in evolutionary terms, as we see it in other mammals such as apes and dogs. When we do something socially unacceptable we can feel a massive threat of being rejected, which can be so devastating that we wish the ground could swallow us up. Situations in which we feel deeply shamed by others can be very traumatic. There is a healthy form of shame, however, that is important for survival in groups. Shameless persons soon lose the respect of others, while shame-sensitive persons feel urged to adapt to the standards of their group. So, even this highly unpleasant emotion can be a friend because it protects the group from antisocial behaviour and ourselves from being expelled. Brené Brown has researched shame extensively and recommends we address this emotion openly, with the courage to be vulnerable.[12]

Guilt

The feeling of guilt is more sophisticated than shame and developed later in evolution, together with the capacity for empathy. We need to understand the effect of our behaviour on others to feel guilty. Whereas the message of shame is '*You* are unacceptable', the message of guilt is 'What you *did* is unacceptable'. Healthy feelings of guilt motivate us to correct mistakes and repair relationships with others. Guilt becomes destructive however, when shame comes on top of it and we judge ourselves unnecessarily harshly for our mistakes. Then, 'I did something bad' becomes 'I am bad'. Strong fears of making mistakes may then develop, blocking the way to learning something new.

Embarrassment and shyness

The message of embarrassment is 'your behaviour is clumsy or stupid'. Feeling shy gives the message 'You had better keep out of the spotlight and give room to others'. It may feel less devastating than shame, but can nonetheless be very disturbing and unpleasant. Whereas shame involves the fear of falling down the social ladder, shyness relates to the fear of moving up the social ladder and standing out too much. In competitive societies people tend to feel ashamed of their shyness, but being shy has great evolutionary advantage. Shyness easily disarms others and helps us to be accepted. Groups function better when not everybody puts themselves to the forefront. Shy people add to the stability of a group. They generally are more socially sensitive and emotionally intelligent than those who are bold.[13]

Envy and jealousy

When someone else has something desirable we may feel envious. Envy's message is 'Others are ahead of you, don't fall behind'. It urges us to be competitive. It can be distinguished from jealousy. We feel jealous when another person gains the interest of someone important to us. We feel urged to bind this person more tightly to us for fear of losing them.

Pride and conceit

Pride gives the message 'You are great, well done' and relates to positive self-evaluation. The healthy side is, that it helps secure our position, the downside is that others become envious of us. And when pride becomes conceit we may well lose their sympathy altogether. When we never feel any healthy pride however, we are more vulnerable to our inner critic.

Don't kill the messengers

So, self-conscious emotions serve our functioning in groups, by regulating our rank and position. They are part of our design as social beings, and ... not our fault! They can become destructive when they are fuelled by new-brain stories telling you are no good. Over-zealous inner critics often misinterpret the messages of self-conscious emotions. They turn them into stories of shame, blame and failure, with which you identify, yielding only more bad feelings and thoughts about yourself and dragging you into vicious spirals of suffering.

If you wish to ease the relationship with your inner critic, a good start is to befriend these self-conscious emotions. They are messengers that evolved to help you survive as a social being. Mindfully recognising them as feelings as they arise and acknowledging self-critical comments as thoughts, not facts, will help you not to over-identify with them. This is how you create a space to compassionately relate to self-conscious emotions and thoughts, listen to the helpful message they may have, while preventing them from polluting your inner environment.

There are many self-critical or otherwise unhelpful stories we can tell about ourselves. The scripts we learned when we were young, can be particularly strong and maladaptive. The next exercise is an example of how you can learn to compassionately relate to these inner patterns.

※ COMPASSIONATELY RELATING TO INNER PATTERNS

Part 1 Recognising inner patterns

Look at the list of 19 sentences below and read through them one by one. Pause after each sentence and give a score in the column Recognisability: 1 = this I don't recognise

continued

---

at all in my life; 2 = this I recognise somewhat; 3 = this I recognise fairly well; 4 = this I recognise well; 5 = this I strongly recognise.

In giving a score, follow your first inclination and pay more attention to the sphere of the sentences than the precise words. Score from what the sentence 'feels' like, instead of giving it a lot of thought.

Inner pattern	Recognisability
1 My close relationships will end because people are unreliable and unpredictable.	1 2 3 4 5
2 I expect that others will hurt me and take advantage of me.	1 2 3 4 5
3 I can't seem to get what I need from others (warmth, attention, understanding, protection, support).	1 2 3 4 5
4 I'm defective, bad, not okay, and don't deserve to be loved by others.	1 2 3 4 5
5 I'm alone in this world, different from others, I do not belong.	1 2 3 4 5
6 I'm boring and totally uninteresting to other people; they don't want me in their company.	1 2 3 4 5
7 I'm not capable of living my life; I need help to take care of myself and to make decisions.	1 2 3 4 5
8 A disaster might happen at any moment, and I won't be able to cope.	1 2 3 4 5
9 I feel empty, confused, lost without guidance from my elders.	1 2 3 4 5
10 I'm a failure, I'm stupid, inept, and will never be successful compared to others.	1 2 3 4 5
11 I deserve whatever I can get; others need to take my wishes into account.	1 2 3 4 5
12 I'm easily frustrated, react impulsively or throw in the towel.	1 2 3 4 5
13 I adapt to what others want from me, out of fear of their anger or rejection.	1 2 3 4 5
14 I suppress my own needs and emotions in order to be of service to others.	1 2 3 4 5
15 For me, everything revolves around getting recognition and appreciation from others.	1 2 3 4 5
16 I presume that whatever can go wrong will go wrong, and that my decisions will not work out.	1 2 3 4 5
17 I prefer not to show my feelings (positive or negative) to others and would rather take a more rational approach.	1 2 3 4 5
18 I'm a perfectionist, need to spend my time efficiently, and abide strictly by the rules.	1 2 3 4 5
19 I'm impatient with others and with myself, and insist that people should be punished for their mistakes.	1 2 3 4 5

(Reproduced and adapted with kind permission from 'My schemas' in C. K. Germer, *The mindful path to self-compassion*. New York: Guilford Press, 2009)

Part 2 Guided meditation exploring an inner pattern

Choose one of the 19 sentences you have given a higher score and that you are willing to explore further in the guided meditation that follows. Read the sentence again and let it resonate inside. Then close your eyes, if you like, mindfully pausing and allowing the breath to find its soothing rhythm.

Now recall a recent situation during which the pattern you just chose was clearly present. Imagine it coming alive again. Were you on your own or with others, what details of the situation are you aware of? Exploring what physical sensations, emotions, thoughts and beliefs are occurring when this pattern is active ... is there anything you try to do or avoid doing, anything you want to say or keep inside, anything you desire or resist...? Do you recognise any specific emotions related to how you see yourself in this situation or how you think others see you? Then reflect on the following questions and see what they touch in you. Don't feel forced to find answers, but trust what emerges by itself. There are no wrong answers. Simply being present with what arises from moment to moment is part of the practice.

- *How and when did this pattern arise in your life? Are there any particular experiences or circumstances at the root of this pattern?*
- *How did the pattern develop itself further? What experiences or circumstances strengthened the pattern in the course of your life?*
- *What about the activity of the emotion regulation systems (threat, drive or soothing) in this pattern? What about a particular stress reaction (fight, flight, freeze or tend and befriend)?*
- *Did and does the pattern have unintended consequences and contribute to your own or others' suffering? If yes, in what ways?*
- *Did you develop this pattern on purpose? To what extent was it an attempt to survive or deal with difficult circumstances?*
- *Has the pattern helped you or has it been beneficial in any way? Is this still so? If yes, how?*
- *How many people on this planet do you think you share this pattern with? A handful? Hundreds? Thousands? Millions?*
- *Could you give the pattern a playful name? Let it be a name that brings a smile to your face, opens your heart and softens your relationship with the pattern.*
- *What could be a compassionate wish to yourself related to this pattern, with regard to the suffering that lies underneath it or the suffering it may cause?*

If a wish came up with the last question you may end the exercise by gently repeating it on the rhythm of the soothing breath.

It may also be fitting to end with the three phrases of the Self-Compassion Mantra, if you wish with a hand on your heart.

1 *'This is suffering.' A pattern is a form of suffering.*
2 *'Suffering is part of life.' Patterns belong to the human condition. You share this pattern with many others.*
3 *'May I be kind to myself here and now.'*

End the exercise in your own time.

You may do this exercise on a number of occasions exploring various inner patterns and use Worksheet 11 for your reflections.

Comfort zones without comfort

The 19 sentences from the previous exercise present a simplified list of so-called schemas.[14] Schemas are patterns that arise at an early age in often difficult circumstances and persist into adulthood where they become maladaptive. As they feel familiar they give a sense of security when life is difficult, a kind of comfort zone, but without real comfort. They keep you in threat or drive mode without soothing you. The roots of these patterns can be quite clear or deeply hidden. They may have been passed on to you by previous generations and the culture you grew up in. Patterns like this are part of life; most people will recognise at least a few. While they may offer protection, they may also cause restriction and make you disapprove of yourself. Disapproval will not make a pattern disappear but will rather cause further suffering as patterns cannot be simply unlearned. They belong to your survival strategies and to your default mode. You slip back into it whenever there is a familiar threat. Just as you will remember how to swim when falling into water, even if it is many years since you last swam. Of course, some patterns may in time fade when you do not feed them. You may have noticed that certain patterns on the list are not as pronounced anymore as they were in the past. You may also have experienced patterns recurring immediately in situations reminiscent of the circumstances in which they developed.

Befriending inner patterns

As inner patterns are difficult to unlearn, we are not suggesting you work really hard to get rid of them. Rather, we recommend that you practise the following:

- Mindfully acknowledging a pattern when it arises, noticing the inner landscape of it: thoughts, feelings, physical sensations.
- Not criticising or fighting the pattern, it only feeds your inner critic – another pattern – and what you resist persists.
- Instead, welcoming the pattern. It may have grown from an intention to help you survive. The situation may be reminiscent of previous difficult phases in your life. Kindly greeting it with a playful name: 'Ah, there you are, Mr Short Fuse … Ugly Duckling … Mrs Perfect … Thank you for coming along. No offence, but today I'll try without your help. You can stay around if you like, just in case you may be needed.' Yes, even a harsh inner critic can be approached like this: 'Welcome, Master Whiplash, have you seen the sun coming out?'
- Asking yourself what would be a compassionate way to respond to this situation. Often it may be wise not to follow the pattern, while at oth-

er moments it may be wise and compassionate to mindfully go along with it, but then with more awareness and understanding.

Friendly teasing is a much kinder activity than bullying. When we bully, there is animosity and no respect. When we tease there is underlying friendship, care and respect; we play and make use of humour, which clears the sky.

Taking a more scenic route

Patterns are like motorways in a landscape. They are well sign posted and have many accesses. As soon as you are on a motorway you can drive at high speed. This is very efficient for getting from A (where you don't want to be) to B (where you want to be), but also very restrictive. For one thing, you cannot stop on a motorway. Also, you move so fast that you miss a lot of the beauty of the landscape. Your mind is focused on the tarmac. It is easy to miss the exits when you mindlessly drive along on autopilot. When a mindful moment makes you realise where you are, you can switch off the autopilot mode, look for an exit and leave the motorway. Then you may find yourself in unknown territory, where there are no fast lanes but only quiet country roads and almost forgotten footpaths, which do not show on your maps or GPS systems. When you try to find your way, nothing is straightforward. You regularly need to pause, observe the landscape and 'feel' your way into it. The speed is slow, enabling you to appreciate the beauty, the challenges and the richness of life outside the 'comfort zone' of your motorway.

This metaphor illustrates what happens in your brain and your behaviour. The neural circuits of inner patterns are like motorways in the brain, heavily used and hard to miss. Stepping out of a familiar pattern is like doing something very unfamiliar. You leave the motorway and try out new behaviour that is not supported by well-trodden neural pathways. But if you learn that this new behaviour proves more helpful, you may well become motivated to repeat it. Remember, that when neurons fire together, they wire together. The neural path will become stronger the more you practise it. This way, you can train your brain to build pathways that support happiness.

Now, let us take a further step into the practice of Kindness Meditation.

※ KINDNESS MEDITATION: A GOOD FRIEND

Start with Kindness Meditation to Yourself as described on p. 20.
Then bring a person to mind who is dear to you, a good friend, partner, parent or grandparent, child or grandchild, a dear colleague or other person who brings a smile to your face and opens your heart.

continued

> *Imagine that the person you chose sits or stands in front of you and you meet their face and eyes... Be aware of how this affects you physically and emotionally... Allow a wish of kindness toward this good friend coming up from your heart... Then gently repeat this wish on the soothing rhythm of the breath... Perhaps in the words that spontaneously came up or in the words of one of the four traditional wishes... 'May you be safe' ... 'May you feel healthy ... happy ... at ease...'*
>
> *You can extend the practice with others in the same category of good friends or persons who are dear to you ... alive or deceased... You can also choose an animal, such as your favourite pet... You can repeat similar or other wishes, which you feel connect well when you imagine this dear one is positioned in front of you and you attune to their deeper needs. Also, a wish in the we-form may be very connecting, e.g. 'May we be free from suffering ... feel peaceful ... share happiness...' Now, it is not about striving to include all dear persons and wishing them every goodness you can think of. Neither is it about achieving results or magic effects. Whether the other person will be affected by your kind wishes can remain an open question. This practice is simply about cultivating an inner attitude of kindness towards somebody dear to you... So, mindfully observing what happens moment by moment... Sometimes you may wish to leave the phrases, just repeating one or two core-words, or simply being present with the atmosphere of kindness and goodwill...*
>
> *If you are noticing emotional heaviness or worrying thoughts, hold them in the cradle of kind awareness, allowing a soothing breathing rhythm to return... You may offer yourself a kind or compassionate wish, only to return to the other person when you feel the space to do so...*
>
> *Continue with this practice as long as you wish.*

※ Calendar: Drive System

Notice moments when the drive system is active. You can note down your observations on the worksheet.

Questions for reflection

– What was the situation?
– How and when did you become aware of the drive system?
– Which physical sensations did you notice?
– Which thoughts and emotions did you notice?
– What are you noticing now, while reflecting on this experience?
– What could be a compassionate response?

SUMMARY CHAPTER 3

In this chapter we explore how we can mindfully and compassionately deal with desires and inner patterns. New-brain and old-brain processes form patterns to help us relate to each other and adapt to specific circumstances. Patterns cause difficulty when repeated in circumstances that require other responses. Three basic patterns are explored in more detail: threat mode, competition mode and caring mode. Furthermore, we look into the nature of the inner critic – a common pattern in relating to ourselves – and how it feeds on self-conscious emotions, like shame and guilt.

SUGGESTIONS FOR PRACTICE

Formal

– Explore one or more desires that easily create suffering with the exercise Compassionately Relating to Desire. 🔊 📝

– Explore a number of inner patterns with the exercise Compassionately Relating to Inner Patterns. 🔊 📝 📝

– Regularly practise Kindness Meditation, extending it to good friends. 🔊

– Continue to practise a Safe Place and a Compassionate Companion.

Informal

– Regularly practise The Breathing Space with Kindness and when you encounter difficulty and painful emotions The Breathing Space with Compassion or The Self-Compassion Mantra.

– Calendar: Drive System. 📝

Notes

1. Homer, *The Odyssey.*
2. Inspired by Brach, T. (2004). *Radical acceptance.* New York: Bantam.
3. Bowen, S., Chawla, N., & Marlatt, A. (2011). *Mindfulness-based relapse prevention for addictive behaviors: A clinician's guide.* New York: Guilford Press.
4. Paraphrasing *I can't get no satisfaction*, a popular song released in 1965 by The Rolling Stones.
5. Goss, K. (2011). *The compassionate mind approach to beating overeating.* London: Constable & Robinson.
6. Gilbert, P. (2000). Social mentalities: Internal 'social' conflicts and the role of inner warmth and compassion in cognitive therapy. In: P. Gilbert & K. G. Bailey (eds), *Genes on the couch: Explorations in evolutionary psychotherapy* (pp.118–150). Hove, UK: Brunner-Routledge.
7. Gilbert, P. (2010). *Compassion focused therapy.* London: Routledge.
8. Neff, K. D., & Vonk, R. (2009). Self-compassion versus global self-esteem: Two different ways of relating to oneself. *Journal of Personality, 77,* 23–50.
9. Jinpa, T. (2015). *A fearless heart: How the courage to be compassionate can transform our lives.* New York: Avery.
10. Ricard, M. (2015). *Altruism: The power of compassion to change yourself and the world.* London: Atlantic.

11. Tracy, J. L., Robins, R. W., & Tangney, J. P. (eds) (2007). *The self-conscious emotions: Theory and research.* New York: Guilford Press.
12. Brown, B. (2012). *Daring greatly.* New York: Gotham.
13. Henderson, L. (2010). *Improving social confidence and reducing shyness using Compassion Focused Therapy.* London: Constable & Robinson.
14. Young, J. E., Klosko, J. S., & Weishaar, M. E. (2003). *Schema therapy: A practitioner's guide.* New York: Guilford Press.

Chapter 4

Out of the mud into the light

Session four: embodying compassion

> *Yesterday I was clever, so I wanted to change the world.*
> *Today I am wise, so I am changing myself.*
>
> —Rumi

In this chapter, we offer some new exercises to help you further explore the inner landscape of kindness and compassion with the help of imagery.

Flow directions of compassion

In the practices you have learned already, you can see that we can play with the direction in which kindness and compassion flow. We can imagine it flowing from another person towards ourselves, or from ourselves toward another person, or even from one part of us to another part of us![1] It is important to practise letting compassion flow in all these directions for it to flourish. Of course, this can also stir up fears (see also Chapter 2). For example, imagining receiving compassion from other people may bring up the fear that they may not be there when we need them in the future, or perhaps that they are only being kind because they want something from us. Letting compassion flow towards other people may induce anxiety that they could take advantage of our generosity, or will overwhelm us with their problems and become dependent on us. Letting compassion flow from ourselves towards ourselves could make us worry about becoming weak and indulgent, or sad and depressed. We may feel unworthy of receiving kindness and believe we do not deserve it.

Now, none of these fears are wrong in any way. It is part of the practice to mindfully hold them in kind awareness, understand them and compassionately respond to them. If you notice that the flow in a specific direction seems blocked, you could experiment with choosing a practice to support the flow in this direction.

We wish to introduce a new exercise in which imagining plays an important role, namely imagining *yourself* as a compassionate person. But before we do this, we invite you to join in a favourite pastime of kids.

Pretend play

We often meet participants who are having problems imagining they can themselves embody compassionate qualities. Allergic reactions and disbelief are not uncommon: 'Me, a compassionate person? Are you kidding? It feels so fake.' Think back to your childhood and how much you enjoyed pretend play. We suggest you try engaging in a little pretend play now.

※ DOING AS IF

We invite you to observe yourself in two short experiments.

Experiment 1

Pretend to be angry for five minutes, pulling an angry face, taking on an angry posture... Really play your role with conviction, getting into the role of being an angry person as best as you can... What do you notice happening in your facial muscles, the rest of your body, your mind, your mood?

Experiment 2

Pretend to be full of joy for five minutes, bringing a smile to your face, letting your body express joy... Embody joy as best as you can, giving yourself up fully to playing this role... Make the whole world believe it ... What do you notice happening in your facial muscles, the rest of your body, your mind, your mood?

Take a moment to reflect on this exercise, using Worksheet 13 to make a few notes about what you experienced.

We have little doubt that you noticed quite different effects with the two experiments, even if you don't think you are a talented actor. If you had a choice, which role to play for the rest of your life, we have little doubt which one you would choose. As already pointed out in Chapter 2, imagination is an important skill in cultivating compassion. If we do not consciously work with our imagination, it is quite likely to work with us while we are unaware of it. Often, it automatically takes us to places that add to our suffering. 'Unreal' images of what we fear or desire can have real effects and cause much unhappiness. The stressful effects of unnecessarily keeping our threat and drive systems going can undermine our health. So, when you imagine being a compassionate person you may not immediately feel like a 'real' one. But when you practise, it may well have some real effects in the body, which are themselves wholesome, not only for yourself but for the people around you. It is not about playing a superficial role without commitment. Play your role as if you are going for an Oscar! Research has shown that just a short daily practice of five minutes for two weeks, imagining a 'Best Possible Self' had beneficial effects on optimism, which is known to contribute to psychological and physical health.[2]

So, here is an exercise to imagine a best possible version of yourself.

※ EMBODYING COMPASSION

Allow yourself to find a comfortable position, either sitting or lying down, and begin with step one and two of the Breathing Space with Kindness...

You are invited to practise with your imagination in a playful way, first allowing a place of safeness coming up, in whatever way it presents itself today, letting all the senses participate... Imagine you are the receiver of kindness from this safe place that surrounds you... Then, in this safe place or independent from it, imagine a compassionate companion emerging, in whatever way it may appear... Envision being the receiver of kindness from another being that accepts you just the way you are and wishes you well... Imagine how this being embodies all qualities of kindness and compassion...

Now imagine you embody compassion yourself, allowing all the qualities you imagined in your compassionate companion also to be present in yourself ... Of course, this is a practice, there is no need to achieve any particular results. Just let your imagination playfully create a compassionate version of yourself, while you mindfully explore what happens. So, imagine...

- *You are deeply sensitive to the needs of others and yourself and committed to relieving suffering and promoting happiness.*
- *You can sympathise – feel with – and empathise – feel into – experiences as they arise, and understand what goes on inside our minds and hearts.*
- *You have the courage to face what is difficult, tolerate suffering and be present with it as long as it needs.*
- *You embody wisdom and a non-judgmental attitude. Having learned from life's lessons, you know how and when to respond in words and deeds. You are patient, allowing space for not-knowing and beginner's mind, opening yourself to new possibilities.*
- *Your whole being is permeated by warmth, kindness, calmness and playfulness.*

While you imagine embodying compassion, also explore what effects it has on you... Explore what happens in your body ... its posture, its feeling tone, its temperature ... in the face, eyes, mouth, throat, chest, belly, arms and legs, allowing your whole body to be involved... And how does this affect your mind and mood state?... All experiences are part of the practice and can mindfully be acknowledged, also your reactivity to the exercise and thoughts like 'I can't do this' or feelings like disappointment or frustration... Mindfully holding these in kind awareness, is already embodying compassion...

continued

> *The more you practise being in the compassionate version of yourself, the more familiar it will become, so be patient with yourself.*
>
> *Mindfully acknowledging whatever arises and returning again and again to the imagery practice of embodying compassion, both in its gentle and powerful qualities... You can also imagine embodying and radiating compassion when you look at something painful in yourself, or something painful in the world around you, like the suffering of another person ... imagining compassion flowing from you to where it is needed.*
>
> *End the practice in your own time, remembering you can always return to it.*

You can note down experiences with this exercise on Worksheet 14.

Questions for reflection

- While imagining yourself as a compassionate being, what sensations did you notice in the body?
- What did you notice in your thoughts and feelings?
- How did embodying compassion affect the inner attitude towards yourself, others and the world around you?
- What are you noticing now, while you reflect on the experience of the exercise?
- When you imagine yourself embodying compassion, what could be a compassionate response to a current difficulty in your life?

The Lotus of Compassion

The lotus flower is an ancient symbol of compassion. The bloom receives nutrition from the mud in which the plant is rooted. The deeper it extends its roots into the mud, the more beautiful the flower. Similarly, the deeper we reach into our suffering, the more our compassion can flourish. As they say in Asia: 'No mud, no lotus'. Here, we blend the symbol of the lotus with insights from Western psychology. It may have become clear that compassion is not one simple entity but an attitude towards suffering made up of different ingredients. These ingredients can be subdivided into attributes and skills. The overview below is based on Paul Gilbert's Circle of Compassion.[3] Inspired by participants in our courses we created the Lotus of Compassion (*Figure 4.1*) out of this. Of course, no model is perfect, but it can help you gain a better understanding of the different aspects involved when training compassion.

- The *heart* of the lotus flower – compassion itself – is revealed when the petals open themselves to the suffering in the world. First, we need to relate and attune to this suffering.
- The inner petals represent the *attributes* of compassion, the specific qualities enabling us to engage with suffering when it arises.

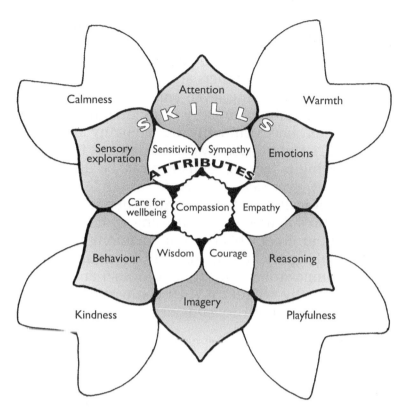

Figure 4.1 The Lotus of Compassion

- Once we can engage with suffering, we can begin to respond to it. The supporting leaves around the inner petals represent the *skills* we need to actively alleviate suffering.
- Compassion cannot thrive in the contraction of threat or drive modes. The four floating leaves represent the right environment in which the lotus can grow and flourish. They represent the *atmosphere* of warmth, calm, kindness and playfulness, the grounding quality of the soothing system.

Below, we list the attributes and skills of compassion one by one. You might like to read through them and ask yourself which ones you could more easily embody and which ones need more practice. Of course, they all reinforce each other and are best cultivated side by side.

Attributes of compassion needed to engage with suffering

- *Care for well-being* – The basic motivation of compassion is to care for ourselves and others and to commit ourselves to alleviating and preventing suffering and promoting happiness wherever we can.
- *Sensitivity* – The ability to sense and attune to what is needed. It requires skilful sensitivity to the needs of others as well as ourselves.
- *Sympathy* – The ability to *feel with* and resonate with each other in joy and sadness. Charles Darwin thoroughly studied this capacity later

in his life, which he considered one of the most successful qualities for survival in higher mammalian species.[4]

- *Empathy* – The ability to *feel into* and understand the inner worlds, motives and behaviours of others and ourselves. Whereas sympathy occurs mainly on the feeling level, empathy also has this cognitive quality of understanding. Empathy is essential in building relationships. Compassion needs empathy, but empathy alone, without the other attributes, is not necessarily compassionate. For example, when care for well-being is lacking, empathy can be used to manipulate others for gain. Clever sales persons for example, can make us buy things we do not really need, just because they seem so 'understanding'. There is also a danger in empathising with others while forgetting to care for ourselves. This is common among those in the caring professions, making them vulnerable to burnout. Matthieu Ricard argued that 'compassion fatigue' is a misnomer and it may be better to speak of 'empathy fatigue'.[5] When compassion flows to where it can relieve suffering, both towards others and ourselves, it should not make us feel tired.

- *Courage and distress tolerance* – Compassion needs both tenderness and strength. It needs courage to meet suffering, especially if it shows itself in its ugliest forms, when we meet our inner demons. We also need courage to be vulnerable and let our hearts be touched. Besides, we need tolerance to endure difficulties as they last.

- *Wisdom* – compassion requires an open mind and respect for the complexity of life and the ability to meet situations with a non-judgmental attitude. When we say 'non-judgmental' we do not mean that you should be without judgments and preferences. Judging can be very helpful in life. Wisdom involves being aware of our judgments and not simply following them on autopilot but aligning them with our intention to relieve suffering and enhance well-being. It also helps us to have patience and a beginner's mind, abiding with the questions if there are no clear answers. Ultimately, wisdom involves discernment between what is helpful and harmful.

Compassionate skills to alleviate suffering can be acquired in the following areas

- *Attention* – mindfulness of experience as it enfolds moment to moment is a key skill. Mindful awareness deepens the quality of what we experience and what we do. In fact, mindfulness is essential to all the skills we list here. Where attention goes, energy flows. So, whatever we give attention grows. If we wish for compassion in all its qualities to grow, we need to choose our field of attention wisely and explore it mindfully.

- *Sensory exploration* – as we have a strong negativity bias by evolutionary design, it requires extra training for the senses to take in the positive. The negativity bias may be useful for survival, but it does not promote happiness. So, it is important to cultivate the skill of taking in what gives us joy, nourishment and energy, through all the senses, by seeing, hearing, smelling, tasting or touching. A simple example of how we can practise this skill is by connecting with the body when we give space to a soothing breathing rhythm.

- *Emotions* – Likewise, we can feed wholesome emotional states such as joy, gratitude and forgiveness. A basic skill is the ability to mindfully step back and hold emotions in open, kind awareness. If they are joyful and uplifting, we can mindfully appreciate and savour them. If they are sad and painful, we can cradle and soothe them in kindness, like a caring mother holding her upset baby. If they are unruly and potentially harmful, we can meet them with equanimity.

- *Reasoning* – mindfulness practice has taught us that trying to change our thoughts by force alone creates more suffering. Mindfully observing our thoughts is an important skill enabling us to open ourselves to other perspectives than the narrow ones of our threat or drive minds. Besides letting our thoughts come and go, we can develop the skill of wisely choosing which ones we listen to and allow to be voiced. It can help us feed those perspectives and arguments that serve to relieve suffering and promote happiness. An example of compassionate reasoning could be 'If you can change it, why worry? If you cannot change it, why worry?' In the next paragraph, we come back to this.

- *Imagery* – the skill of working with compassionate and wholesome imagery, like imagining a Safe Place, a Compassionate Companion, or Embodying Compassion. These imagery practices can act like an internal medicine against the toxic effects of images of fear and hate.

- *Behaviour* – Speaking and behaving compassionately, with respect, non-violence and kindness, is what many religions and wisdom traditions have encouraged us to do. The Golden Rule 'Treat others as you wish to be treated yourself' is one of the greatest achievements of humankind. It has inspired universal behavioural codes such as the Declaration of Human Rights. It is an important skill to behave in line with these universal guidelines, while at the same time listening to the wisdom of our hearts in specific situations.

Feeding an inner helper

In the previous chapter, we tried to understand why we so easily develop an inner critic or even an inner bully. In this chapter, we further expand on how you can cultivate an inner helper. This requires a lot of practice as the design of our brain is, by no fault of our own, primarily aimed at immediate survival (threat or drive mode) rather than sustainable well-being (caring mode). In the previous paragraph, we mentioned wholesome reasoning as one of the skills of compassion. Below, we compare the perspective of an inner critic or bully with the perspective of an inner helper.

Inner critic	Inner helper
• Biased towards negativity	• Open towards experience as it is
• Seeing failures and shortcomings: *What went wrong, is wrong, will go wrong*	• Seeing growth and development: *What went well, goes well, is possible*
• Punitive towards the past	• Forgiving towards the past
• Mistrustful towards the future	• Encouraging towards the future
• Harsh, impatient, humiliating attitude	• Kind, patient, supportive attitude
• Intolerant of what went wrong and blaming you for mistakes	• Trying to understand what went wrong and inviting you to learn from mistakes
• Attacking you as a *person*	• Addressing your *behaviour*
• Evoking shame and fear of rejection	• Evoking healthy guilt and remorse
• Causing worries about consequences for yourself	• Raising concern about consequences for all involved
• Making you feel irritable and anxious, avoiding or resisting contact	• Helping you take up responsibilities, make amends and heal relationships

What differs is not just the content of their ways of thinking but also their attitude and feeling tone. These can be as far apart as the different styles of a critical, impatient teacher humiliating and punishing a child with learning difficulties, versus a kind and caring teacher who would be patient, caring and supporting. If it were your child you would surely trust it to a school with caring teachers. Still, many of us find it difficult to cultivate a kind inner teacher. If the left column looks far more familiar to you than the right column, do not despair. Being able to mindfully recognise our patterns in thoughts, feelings and behaviours is an important first step towards change. This enables us to stop feeding the inner critic and start empowering an inner helper as a healthier way of relating to ourselves.

In the first three sessions of the MBCL course we presented a lot of new exercises and background information. Exercises that focus on our inner difficulties, such as resistances, desires and inner patterns, can be quite demanding. To create more spaciousness, we keep the fourth session somewhat lighter, cultivating kindness and compassion based on already familiar practices. Here is another extension of the Kindness Meditation, widening the circle of compassion to neutral persons.

※ KINDNESS MEDITATION: A NEUTRAL PERSON

After having practised kindness meditation towards ourselves, a benefactor and persons dear to us, we now expand our practice towards 'neutral' persons. It is quite unusual to feel exactly neutral towards others, as when we look at them more closely, subtle sympathetic or antipathetic feelings often arise. What is meant is that we chose a person we do not know very well and feel impartial towards, such as somebody you just happened to meet and with whom you have or seek no special relationship – a passer-by in your life. Perhaps somebody you saw at the bus stop or waiting next to you for the traffic lights.

If you have found a neutral person, you may imagine this person in front of you, realising he or she is just like you a human being wishing for happiness and vulnerable to suffering... Then begin to gently repeat wishes of kindness to that person, such as 'May you (or we) feel safe ... happy ... at ease', on the rhythm of the breath or independently from it... Mindfully observe what happens while you practise... You can gradually include other persons or animals belonging to this neutral category.

Here also, it is not about doing this practice with as many neutral beings as you can think of, which might be a relief because they are countless. It is about cultivating a sensitive heart to others whom you have no particular relationship with, but who nonetheless cross your path. If you notice your attention drifts or you encounter inner difficulties, you can always return to self-compassion and return to neutral others when you feel the space to do so.

And as one of the themes of this chapter is embodying compassion, we would like to offer some exercises expanding body awareness and mindful movement, building on familiar mindfulness practices.

※ KINDNESS FOR THE BODY

You are invited to lie down in a comfortable position on a surface that is neither too hard nor too soft. Take care you are warm enough; allow the breath to settle in a soothing rhythm, the body to surrender to gravity and the muscles to soften.

Now connect with a part of your body you feel contented and at ease with. It may be because it is strong, healthy or good-looking or because it is a reliable companion, functions well or gives you joy. Notice how this part feels and sense what it needs ... Then, allow a kind wish to flow to it. In the same way as you can send kindness to a person you have a good relationship with, you can also direct kindness to a bodily part you have a good relationship with, as if it were a person – whatever your rational mind may think of it. You could use phrases like: 'May you feel healthy and happy ... feel relaxed and cared for ... enjoy the goodness of life...', or whatever connects well... Allow the breath to support you, for instance by breathing towards and attuning to this part on the in-breath ('May you...'), and by letting kindness flow towards it on the out-breath ('... feel happy') or in another way that feels natural to you... Explore both the giving and receiving aspects of this practice. How is the wish received in this part? ... Do not hesitate to change the words and adapt your inner attitude to facilitate it being accepted... Likewise, you can include other parts of the body with which you have a good relationship and treat these to kind wishes.

Rest a while in soothing breath, then connect with a bodily part with which you have a fairly neutral relationship. This might be because it mostly goes unnoticed and you do not see or feel it very often. Gently attune to this part on the rhythm of the breath and let words of kindness flow to it. For example, 'May you be accepted', 'May you belong to the body as a whole' or 'I wish you happiness'... Notice how the wish is received... Continue with other parts to which you feel relatively neutral.

continued

Allow your attention again to rest on the breath and – if necessary – allow a soothing rhythm to return. Then connect with a part of your body you have a difficult relationship with. It may be because you feel uncomfortable or ashamed about it, you find it unattractive when you see it in the mirror, or it malfunctions and is vulnerable, a source of pain or illness. Maybe it was injured or it had surgery. Choose a part like this and observe what is there to be experienced right now... Do you sense what its deeper needs are? Then allow a compassionate wish to flow to this part, on the soothing rhythm of the breath, e.g. 'May you feel as healthy as can be ... have courage ... be strong and bear with this suffering' or 'I wish you comfort ... kindness ... all the care you need...' Sensing how it is received ... do not hesitate to alter the words if necessary. Noticing your thoughts and feelings in open, kind awareness, while sending kindness to this bodily part ... allowing space for painful emotions and sadness ... continue as you wish, with the same or another part with which you have a difficult relationship.

You can conclude this practice by expanding your awareness to your body as a whole, holding it in an embrace of kindness and compassion. Realise how this body has been your companion all your life, in joyful and in difficult times... As you can have good, neutral and difficult relationships with various members of your family, so you can have variable relationships with different parts of your body. Include all these parts in your caring embrace and offering kindness and gratitude to this body as if it were one family, with all the qualities, vulnerabilities and imperfections of its various members. 'May you feel safe ... as healthy as can be ... strong and courageous ... whole and peaceful...'

Return to this practice as often as you wish, It can be a powerful way to cultivate a healing relationship with your body.

Mindful movement

Practising kindness towards the body during rest can be continued while the body is moving. You can deepen mindful movement exercises or yoga as practised in basic mindfulness courses by explicitly cultivating the inner attitude of kindness. Gently self-massaging or tapping your face and body can deepen sensory exploration. While you do this you can observe what happens on the giving and on the receiving side. When you do mindful stretch or yoga movements you can observe how the breath responds to the movements. You can also playfully let the breath guide the movements. Start from a soothing breathing rhythm, letting the movements follow the breath, starting small and making them bigger as breathing becomes deeper. You may explore movement practices that are gentle and soft in nature like Qi Gong and Tai Chi, or follow the suggestions offered in programmes like Breathworks,[6] which are designed for those who suffer from chronic pain and physical restrictions.

Below, we give examples of how we can offer some playful mindful movement practice during a session.

※ EXAMPLES OF MINDFUL MOVEMENT

Expanding the heart

- Stand upright with your feet slightly more than hip-width apart, your knees and ankles soft and somewhat bent, your lower arms crossed in front of your lower abdomen, right over left.
- Move your elbows upward on an in-breath, as if you are pulling off a jumper over your head.

Stretch the body gently, raising your arms above your head.

- Moving your arms sideways and downwards on the out-breath, bouncing back through your knees, and returning into the starting position, now with your lower arms crossed left over right.

Repeat the exercise several times alternating the ways you cross the arms. Observe the body while you move, particularly noticing what occurs in the region of your heart. Quite often, people notice a desire to yawn during stretches like this. This is perfectly fine. Yawning is a healthy sign of feeling at ease and coming into your soothing system.

Gently swinging and bouncing

- Start from the basic standing position, slowly rotating the body back and forth, pushing alternately from the left and the right foot, allowing the arms and the whole body to follow loosely, without effort. Let a comfortable rhythm and movement width arise by itself... Continue for a couple of minutes, noticing the sensations in the body... Then let the swinging fade out, resting in the standing position, being aware of your experience moment by moment.
- Then begin to gently bounce through your knees and ankles, allowing the whole body to loosely follow, finding a comfortable rhythm, as if you are riding an animal... It may start at a slow elephant pace, then gently becoming faster, if you like as fast as a Shetland pony at full speed... You can continue for a few minutes at a comfortable pace, letting the movements gradually fade and coming to a standstill... Notice the energy flowing through the body, including any sensations in the palms of your hands.

Giving and receiving

- On an in-breath, move your arms and hands sideways until your fingers touch above your head, palms downward, as if they form the head of a shower... Imagine a shower of light, warmth or healing energy coming out of the palms of your hands, which your body receives.
- On an out-breath, gently move your hands downward along your body, at close distance without touching ... first head and face, then neck, chest and belly until they return to the resting position, holding the arms loosely alongside the body.
- Repeat this a number of times, alternately paying attention to the giving and receiving aspects of this practice and allowing your hands to travel different routes along the body.

Walking meditation is usually practised in basic mindfulness courses at a slow pace. Here is a way to deepen mindful walking with kindness.

※ WALKING WITH KINDNESS

We can also deepen walking meditation by combining it with kindness meditation. Find yourself a suitable place, indoors or outdoors, where you can walk up and down or in a circle.

Begin with mindfully noticing the body while it rests in a standing position, allowing the feet to be placed firmly on the ground hip-width apart, the ankles and knees to be soft, the body, neck and head upright without effort, the arms loosely alongside. Allow your gaze to rest a few metres in front of you. Kindly notice bodily sensations, mood, thoughts and feelings.

Then start to walk, allow a soothing walking rhythm to develop, a rhythm that calms the body and the mind. Depending on inner and outer circumstances, this rhythm may vary, e.g. when you feel warm it may be slower than when you feel cold. It may be helpful to allow the breath to settle comfortably in this soothing walking rhythm, without forcing... Kindly notice the moving body while you walk... Then ask yourself 'What could be a kind wish to myself right now?'... If nothing in particular comes up, you can practise with one of the traditional wishes for feeling safe, healthy, happy or at ease. Gently repeat the phrase, allowing the words to flow naturally with the rhythm of your footsteps. Depending on the pace, you can repeat the whole sentence with every step, e.g. 'May I feel calm', or just the core word 'calm' with every step, or 'May' with the placing of your left foot, 'I' with the right foot, 'feel' with left, 'calm' with right, and so on... As long as repeating the words is helpful, just continue... If you feel you are immersed in a calm atmosphere, you can leave the words and just mindfully appreciate what you notice ... repeating them again when they support you... It is not about striving for effects, but about cultivating kind intentions towards yourself... You can keep practising with one wish, but can also shift to another one if you feel this connects better. If connecting the phrase with your footsteps confuses you, just repeat the wish independently from your steps.

You can expand this practice by sending kind wishes to others coming up in your thoughts, e.g. a benefactor, a dear or a neutral person... When you practise where you are not alone, you can also send kindness to people or animals that come up in your visual or hearing field. You do not need to seek eye-contact. Here also, it is not so much about achieving effects, but about cultivating an inner attitude of kindness to those you happen to meet. This can be a playful and wholesome practice in the category of neutral beings, with whom you do not have a special relationship, sending kindness to passers-by in your life, wherever you go.

※ Calendar: Inner Critic

Notice when the inner critic is present. Now, do not criticise yourself for your inner critic, but ask yourself what a compassionate response could be. You can make notes on the worksheet.

Questions for reflection

- What was the situation?
- How did you become aware of the inner critic?
- What did the inner critic say to you?
- What did you notice in your body and emotions?
- What are you noticing now, while reflecting on this experience?
- What could be a compassionate response?

SUMMARY CHAPTER 4

In this chapter we map out attributes, skills and the atmosphere that supports compassion in the Lotus of Compassion. We discuss how we can cultivate an inner helper, embody compassion with the help of imagery and expand familiar mindfulness practices, such as the body scan, mindful moving and mindful walking with kindness practice.

SUGGESTIONS FOR PRACTICE

Formal

- Try the Doing as If exercise.
- Regularly practise Embodying Compassion.
- Expand the Kindness Meditation with neutral persons.
- Explore Kindness for the Body, Mindful Movement (p. 70–71) and/or Walking with Kindness.
- Do formal practices from previous chapters as required.

Informal

- Regularly practise the Breathing Space with Kindness and when you encounter difficulty and painful emotions the Breathing Space with Compassion or the Self-Compassion Mantra.
- Calendar: Inner Critic.

Notes

1. For the flow directions of compassion and their blocks, see: Gilbert, P. (2009). *The compassionate mind.* London: Constable & Robinson; Jinpa, T. (2015). *A fearless heart.* New York: Avery.
2. Meevissen, Y. M. C., Peters, M. L., & Alberts, H. J. M. E. (2011). Become more optimistic by imagining a best possible self: Effects of a two week intervention. *Journal of Behavior Therapy and Experimental Psychiatry, 42,* 371–378.
3. Gilbert, P. (2009). *The compassionate mind.* London: Constable & Robinson. For didactic reasons we have given wisdom and courage a clearer

place in the model, where Gilbert puts the attributes of non-judgement and distress tolerance. Wisdom entails both non-judgement and discernment. Courage combines both readiness to face the difficult and endurance to bear with it.

4. Darwin's interest in sympathy is highlighted in Keltner, D. (2009). *Born to be good*. New York: W.W. Norton.
5. Ricard, M. (2015). *Altruism*. London: Atlantic.
6. Burch, V., & Penman, D. (2013). *Mindfulness for health: A practical guide to relieving pain, reducing stress and restoring wellbeing*. London: Piatkus.

Chapter 5

Receiving and giving with every breath

Session five: self and others – widening the circle

If you want to go fast, go alone.
If you want to go far, go with others.

—African proverb

You are now halfway through this book. Just take a moment to reflect on the first half of the course. What have you learned? What effects have you noticed in your life? Kindly notice whatever arises during this reflection, whether blessings, insights, struggles, disappointments or doubts. Let your experience be just as it is. What would you wish for yourself from the second half of the course?

'Dear Self'

In this session, we will further explore how we can cultivate kindness in relating to ourselves and others. How can we compassionately respond when meeting suffering? We may become more sensitive to the needs of others when we first learn to sense the needs of the suffering parts in ourselves. We invite you to explore this further in the next exercise, for which you will need pen and paper.

※ A COMPASSIONATE LETTER

First, make yourself comfortable and follow the instructions of the exercise Embodying Compassion as described in the previous chapter, p. 63. Take the time you need to feel connected with the compassionate version of yourself, before you continue.

Now, choose an area in your life that you experience as difficult or painful. Kindly choose something you feel you can face right now. It may be a situation you encoun-

continued

---

tered recently or some while ago, which still causes distress. Perhaps it was dominated by painful emotions or harsh self-criticism. While you imagine embodying compassion in all its qualities, look at the suffering version of yourself in that situation. Imagine you are looking at it from your compassionate self, with a deep motivation to alleviate its suffering. Do you see an anxious, angry, sad, lonely or confused version of yourself? What is the facial expression and posture of this suffering self? How does it behave? Let there be kindness in your gaze while you look at this suffering self. Be sensitive to its needs. What qualities of compassion are asked for? It may be tenderness, warmth and comfort, or courage and strength, or patience and understanding. What would be a wise, compassionate response? Hold the difficulties and questions as they arise. There may be no easy answers. Allow for not-knowing, being with whatever arises, until the right response shows itself.

Now, begin to write a letter to your suffering self, the 'you' who is addressed, from your compassionate self, the 'I' who is writing. Allow the words to come as they come. Do not force anything. This practice can be held in a light and playful manner. If you lose the connection with your compassionate self, kindly acknowledge what arises, including doubt, insecurity or resistance against the practice. Allow the breath to soothe you and if you begin to feel more space, return to imagining that you embody compassion. Let the words flow from a calm place. Maybe it is not a very coherent story that comes out, but rather keywords or short sentences, metaphors or even drawings. Allow yourself to be surprised what arises and expresses itself in the letter. If you find it difficult to connect with your compassionate self, you can perhaps find inspiration by imagining how a compassionate companion would relate to your suffering self. Remember it is a practice, not a test.

After ten minutes or so, take a break and read what you have written so far. Does the content have the qualities of compassion? Sense how it is received by your suffering self. Notice how your suffering self responds to the style, words and images. Maybe you notice subtle judgments or criticisms, 'shoulds' or 'oughts' that have unintentionally crept in. Well done! Recognising the ways in which an inner critic can show up, perhaps in disguise, is an important part of the practice. Compassionately respond to whatever arises. Your suffering self can offer valuable feedback. How does it need to be seen and addressed? Do not hesitate to change, adjust or expand your letter. Is there anything missing in the letter that your suffering self really needs to hear? What about adding a final sentence or core message?

You can extend this practice by imagining reading the letter aloud to your suffering self. Imagine you are embodying compassion while you do this. How is the posture of your body, your facial expression, the gaze of your eyes? How is the tone and rhythm of your voice? If you are alone, you do not have to pretend but can actually read it aloud. Can you sense what is needed in your attitude that allows your suffering self to open and receive the message? And how is it received? It may be helpful to see yourself in a mirror. If you find it difficult to identify both with the reader and the listener at the same time, you can make a recording while you embody compassion and listen to it later while identifying with your suffering self. Allow for creativity in this practice. Explore what it takes to enable an intimate, healing connection in yourself between giving and receiving compassion.

It may be tempting to do this practice quickly. It may feel difficult, unfamiliar or childish. Don't worry, it is not meant to be an exam. It is just another form of practice. The invitation is to openly explore it and return to it whenever it might be helpful. We all have our preferences for certain practices. In the first session of a mindfulness course, some people immediately fall in love with the body scan while others hate it. Still, the practices we dislike at first, might be the ones that give us powerful insights when we return to them with kind curiosity. Allow yourself time to write a compassionate letter on different occasions, addressing different inner difficulties. First, connect with embodying compassion or with a compassionate companion before picking up your pen. Many participants, who first felt resistance, discover how healing this exercise can be. On the other hand, as with any practice, there are no right or wrong experiences. Mindfully noting what arises, pleasant or unpleasant, already opens the space for new discoveries and insights. Here are some questions and suggestions for extra support.

Questions for reflection

While practising compassionate letter writing, you may ask yourself: Does the letter express ...

- sensitivity, does it acknowledge the pain of the suffering self? For example, 'I see the tears in your eyes', 'I hear the trembling in your voice' or 'I sense the tension in your shoulders'.
- sympathy, does it resonate with what the suffering version of yourself is going through? For example, 'It touches my heart to see you like this. I really feel for you.'
- empathy, does the letter offer understanding of the feelings, thoughts and behaviours of the suffering self? For example, 'Of course, you felt disappointed when your friend did not call. I can see that you had dark thoughts of being unworthy. It must remind you of past experiences when you felt abandoned. I can understand you had to comfort yourself and rolled yourself up in a blanket.'
- courage and strength to face and hold what is difficult? For example, 'I am here and will stand right at your side if you wish. I am not afraid of painful emotions, I know them well. They hurt, but they can teach us how to grow in patience and resilience. We do not have to wallow in them, but we do not have to block them out either. Let's just listen to what they have to say.'
- a genuine motivation to care for the well-being of the suffering self? Does the letter express wisdom, not just in what is said, but also how it is said? Is the basic attitude open-minded, non-judgmental and playful? For example, 'I wish there was a way to ease your pain. Let me know if there is anything you need. Just being with what's here right now, might be all that's needed. Let's be patient and watch the mud settle until the water becomes clear... Do you remember how you were comforted before by listening to this song... by taking a sauna... by stroking your dog... by cracking jokes with your little nephew? I really wish you find out what serves you best. There is no need to force anything, just try when you feel ready.'

Variations

- If you find it difficult to connect with your compassionate self, you can write a letter from your compassionate companion. What words and what tone would this compassionate companion choose?
- You can write a compassionate letter to your inner critic or one of the patterns that you recognised in the previous chapter. Allow for creativity, playfulness and humour. For instance, 'My dearest Inner Bully...' or 'Honourable Mrs Perfect...' or 'Dear Workaholic, I beg your pardon for taking some of your precious time...' If you feel a lot of resistance with a writing exercise like this, you can address the difficulty in yourself that is facing you right now: 'Dear Resistance...'
- If you keep a diary, you may integrate compassionate writing there. Begin with embodying compassion before you start. One of our participants, who was a keen rapper, noticed how the words changed, when rapping from his compassionate self.
- Finally, you can also address a compassionate letter to another person. Somebody who is dear to you and whom you are concerned about. Or somebody you have a difficult relationship with. This does not mean you must actually send the letter. It is, foremost, a practice for yourself, exploring how your compassionate self might respond to someone else.

Who are *you?*[1]

The previous exercise may have given you a sense of what we call 'identification'. Often, we are not aware that our minds are busy identifying or 'selfing'. From an early age we learn to divide the world into 'me' and 'not-me'. Identifications give us a sense of security in given circumstances. Just try making a shopping list or booking a ticket without identifying yourself with your needs. Or try going to work being 'Nobody'. You would risk being fired. We need to identify with our roles and tasks, otherwise we cannot function. But identifications can also restrict us and stand in the way. Particularly, when we identify with a fixed self-image or 'ego', which we hold on to, no matter what the circumstances are.

As the writer of the letter you were invited to identify with a compassionate self and as the receiver of the letter with a suffering self. We may think we refer to a solid self every time we say 'I', 'me' or 'mine', but what we refer to with these tiny words is not always the same. The quality of the relationship with ourselves depends very much on the part of ourselves we look *from* and the part of ourselves we look *at*. Our inner weather state can change dramatically when we look *from* a critical self, an indifferent self or a loving self, or when we look *at* a failing self, a boring self or a successful self.

Perhaps the following story will give you a better idea of what we mean.

The Castaway

A castaway is fighting for his life in rough seas. Becoming very exhausted, he manages to grab a piece of driftwood. He can keep his head above water with less effort and catch his breath. When the sea calms down, he feels how cold he is and he begins to look around.

After a while, he sees a large barrel floating in the distance. He decides to let go of the driftwood and swims to the barrel. He can lift himself onto it. The driftwood is already forgotten and he feels his body warming up in the sun. When hours have passed, he realises how serious his situation is. He is drifting all alone on this barrel in a vast ocean. After a long time, he spots an empty lifeboat that must have become dislodged from the ship before it sank. Without deliberation, he lets go of the barrel and swims in the direction of the lifeboat. He has already completely forgotten about the barrel when he manages to seize the boat and climbs on board. How fortunate! Even the oars are in the boat and a small parcel of emergency provisions. He eats and drinks and his strength returns. He starts to row in the direction where he suspects there might be land.

Finally, his effort is rewarded. He reaches an island. He pulls the boat that saved him onto the beach. In the distance, he spots a village and begins to walk. He deeply longs for human contact and has already forgotten about the boat...

The problem with over-identifying

When I let go of what I am, I become what I might be.
—Lao Tzu

Would it not be tragic if you were a castaway clinging to a piece of driftwood, while missing the lifeboat that drifts by! Just let the idea sink in that your ego is just a survival tool. Although your ego may pretend to be indispensable, it is just a construct of your mind. Like all constructs, it is impermanent. It may be temporarily useful, but in need of revision if the circumstances change. The driftwood, the barrel and the boat in the story can be viewed as metaphors for the different forms the ego can take. Temporarily, they may be very useful, even life-saving, but there comes a time when it is better to let go of them, so you can take hold of something else. Both identifying and dis-identifying can be healthy processes. Over-identifying can be stressful and energy intensive, however. Psychological health involves being flexible in your identifications. It can help you survive, grow and thrive.

'What about my true self?'

You might be thinking 'Hang on, I definitely sense some sort of continuity over time. This *me* living in *my* body when *I* was a toddler, a child, a teenager and now an adult, surely it has always been there? Is this ongoing something not my true self?' You are right, we cannot deny this sense of 'self', of being the 'experiencer' of our experiences and the 'identifier' who identifies. You can call this your 'true self', if you like. But does it really have a fixed identity? It is, rather, a flexible or even 'empty' self, which fills itself with different content as life progresses.[2]

'Selfing' on autopilot or by choice

If we are not mindful of this process of identification, it can operate on autopilot. Then it can cause a lot of suffering. When seas are rough and waves are huge, we understandably grab the first thing that saves us from drowning. When seas are calm, it is healthier to broaden our perspective and allow space for new possibilities. This may be hard, particularly when the turbulent seas of threat and competition modes have become 'normal' life to us. If we are over-identified with the mental pictures we made of ourselves or the stories we tell about ourselves, we easily get stuck in rigid patterns and unhappy relationships, both with ourselves and others.

Having restrictive views of the 'selfs' of others can be just as harmful, as we may just see their piece of driftwood and overlook their potential. The quality of relationships we have with others depends on the part of ourselves we look *from* and the part of the other we look *at*. There is a world of difference between looking from a blaming self toward a failing other and looking from a compassionate self toward a suffering other. So, it would be better to calm the turbulent seas of strong emotions and judgment first by giving space to the soothing system and opening our minds and hearts.

Embodying compassion is a valuable practice to return to again and again, also when you practise Kindness Meditation. Let the kind wishes flow from your compassionate self, whether you address yourself or another person in their suffering. Here is the next step of the Kindness Meditation if you are feeling ready to practise with a more challenging person. This category is generally referred to as the 'difficult' person. Note the inverted commas, however. We do not suggest this person 'is' difficult, we just mean you experience the relationship with that person as difficult.

※ KINDNESS MEDITATION: A 'DIFFICULT' PERSON

Resentment is like taking poison and waiting for the other person to die.
—Unknown source

Start with step 1 and 2 of the Breathing Space with Kindness and imagine you embody compassion. If you wish, you can repeat kindness to yourself, a benefactor, dear or neutral persons, allowing kind wishes to flow on the rhythm of the breath...

Then move on to a person you have difficulty with. Be kind to yourself and don't start with your worst enemy! Choose someone you somehow feel uneasy with and feel the space to practise with. It might be someone who criticised you, ignored you, or treated you disrespectfully. Remember that this practice is not about condoning bad behaviour. It is about alleviating suffering, including your own. Feelings of anger, hate and resentment cause much unhappiness, not in the least for yourself. So, it may be helpful to start this practice by embodying compassion and realising we are all imperfect and vulnerable human beings.

Now visualising this person at a safe distance in front of you ... can you imagine looking him or her in the eyes? Realise that this person is a human being longing for happiness and freedom from suffering, like yourself. He or she was once a small innocent child and has probably encountered pain and sorrow in their lives, now trying to live in a frantic world, just like yourself... Just see if you can send a kind wish to this person, a wish without self-interest... For example, 'May you feel safe ... free from suffering ... at peace...' Be mindful of inner reactions when you repeat the wish. You do not have to feel comfortable with it. It is quite normal for suppressed emotional pain to surface. Feelings of being hurt, wronged or neglected may make it difficult to carry on. Mindfully acknowledge what arises and work kindly and patiently with any resistance. Don't hesitate to shift the practice back to self-compassion. After all, you may be the person who needs kindness most right now. When you feel there is enough space again, you may return to the difficult person. If the resistance persists, continue with self-compassion or choose someone less difficult. A wish in the we-form may also give space: 'May we feel safe' or 'May we be at ease'. Likewise, you can practise with other persons you find it difficult to get on with.

When you finish, don't forget to appreciate yourself for this practice, which takes courage. A special way to end, is to imagine gathering around you all the people from the different categories you practised with. Imagine you are sitting in a circle with one or more benefactors, dear, neutral and difficult persons and offer kind wishes to all, including yourself, as a group: 'May we feel safe ... healthy ... happy ... at ease. May there be peace and harmony for all of us.'

Notes on Kindness Meditation

We have introduced Kindness Meditation step by step, starting with yourself, followed by a benefactor and dear, neutral and difficult persons. This sequence is usually followed in Buddhist traditions, where it is called *Metta* or the practice of Loving Kindness.[3] It goes on with sending kindness to smaller and larger groups, and eventually to all beings. You do not have to be a Buddhist or religious person to do this kind of practice. It can be helpful to anyone. In this compassion training course, designed for other settings, we chose to teach a more flexible and accessible form that can easily be followed without being disrespectful to any traditions. We have therefore simply called it Kindness Meditation, or sometimes – with a respectful wink – *Metta 'light'*. The addition 'light' should not be misunderstood as requiring less serious practice. It just means the form and dose is compassionately adjusted to the needs of those who practise in secular, non-religious settings.

Kindness Meditation can be practised boundlessly, unlimited by time or space. All humans, animals or other beings – past, present and future – can be included. This may seem a bit over the top. But it is not like a computer game, striving for ever higher levels, or boosting your ego by becoming an Olympic champion of kindness sports. It is a mindfulness-based practice inviting you to curiously explore what happens when you work with different categories. Let it be an open question whether your practice will have effect on others. In any case, it can nourish the soothing system and deepen the insight in your own mind and heart. This can be surprisingly wholesome. Barbara Fredrickson, who showed the positive effects of Loving Kindness Meditation in her research, refers to 'love' as 'a micro-moment of positivity resonance'.[4] When we experience love, then our brains, hearts and bodies respond in tune with each other and with the other person. You can even experience it for a fleeting second when you exchange a smile with a stranger. Even if you do not see the real person, Kindness Meditation can be beneficial for yourself and your inner attitude towards the other person. And this may also affect the relationship in a positive way when you meet the person in real life.

Challenges in Kindness Meditation

When practising with different categories of people, you can have quite different experiences and encounter specific difficulties. These may uncover areas in yourself in need of kindness. You will not be surprised if this happens with the difficult person, but it can happen with all categories. So, do not hesitate to go back to compassionate wishes to yourself, again and again and cultivate your inner positivity resonance with the suffering parts in you. When you reconnect with the calmness of the soothing system, you may feel the space to return to others again.

The table on the next page lists some guidelines that may help you 'troubleshoot' when you practise Kindness Meditation with different categories.

A wordless alternative

For it is in giving that we receive.
—St Francis of Assisi

Some people find it difficult to connect with the wishes of Kindness Meditation or find the words lose their meaning after a while. Here is a practice that can be a refreshing alternative. It does not need words and is derived from an ancient Tibetan tradition, where it is called *Tonglen,* meaning 'receiving-giving'.[5] We have renamed it 'Compassionate Breathing', or *Tonglen 'light'*, as – like *Metta* – we offer it in a more accessible way for secular settings. It will take some courage, as it invites you to engage with suffering in an intimate way. At the same time, you can take it lightly and playfully, allowing yourself space to work with what you can handle.

Kindness to …	When you start	What may be difficult	What may be helpful
Benefactor	– Choose someone whom you deeply appreciate for their wisdom and kindness. – You do not need to have a personal relationship and he/she does not need to be perfect. – A beloved pet or innocent child is fine too.	– Worry about the person's health or fear of losing the person. – Sadness because the person is far away or has died.	– Mindfully acknowledging whatever arises. – Returning to self-compassion whenever you encounter suffering in yourself. – Allowing a soothing breathing rhythm, a smile on your face, a hand on your heart.
Dear person or good friend	– Begin with a dear person that brings a smile to your face. – Continue with others, but don't strive to include everyone who is dear to you, it is just a practice.	– Worry about the person's well-being. – Envy if the person is somehow more fortunate than you. – Irritation if the person overlooked your needs.	– Imagining you embody compassion in all its qualities. – Returning to the other only if you feel the space to do so.
Neutral person	– Your feeling does not have to be exactly neutral. – Choose any 'passer-by' in your life or in your mind, others can follow.	– Boredom – Indifference – Drowsiness – Impatience	– Visualising the other at a comfortable distance. – Imagining you are looking at the other person's face and into their eyes.
'Difficult' person	– Choose someone you feel you can face right now. – Realise this person is vulnerable and imperfect, like yourself. – You do not have to condone bad behaviour.	– Resistance – Emotional pain, anger, anxiety, grief, thoughts and feelings of being wronged.	– Reflecting on common humanity: e.g. 'This person wishes to be free from suffering, like me'.
Groups of humans or animals	– Start with groups you belong to, then move on to others. – You may 'zoom in' by visualising an individual of the group whose face you know (if only from the TV or a photo), then 'zoom out' again.	– Feeling overwhelmed by the intensity of people's suffering from war, poverty or natural disaster. – Feeling hopeless or powerless.	– Alternating between you- and we-form, e.g. 'May we live in harmony'. – Alternating with the practice of other heart qualities, e.g. sympathetic joy, when you feel envious; equanimity, when you feel overwhelmed (see Chapters 6 and 7).
All beings	– Start from realising that all beings are vulnerable to illness, ageing and dying and seek to ease their suffering and fulfil their needs.	– Feeling insignificant or disconnected in the vastness of the universe.	– Alternate with Compassionate Breathing (see page 84–85).

※ COMPASSIONATE BREATHING: YOURSELF

Find a comfortable sitting position. Like other practices, Compassionate Breathing starts from mindful presence and the calmness of a soothing breath... Your mind being like a bright mirror, reflecting whatever shows itself... Allow a soothing breathing rhythm to emerge ... returning to it again and again, whenever you notice you have lost it during the practice. There is no need to force the breath. 'Allowing' is the keyword here ... allowing the breath to flow freely in and freely out ... allowing the body to open all its pores to receive, let itself be filled, and give away... Every breath cycle in effortless exchange with the environment ... a welcoming and an offering... And if you notice the energy of threat or drive, resisting or striving, allowing mindful presence and soothing breathing to return...

Now, choose an area of suffering in your life, something you feel the space to work with right now... It may be a physical or an emotional pain. Allow your imagination to play with this. Imagine this pain occupies space and is situated in front of you... What do you imagine it looks like ... what visual qualities does it have, what colour, what shape? What other sensory qualities do you imagine it has? How does it feel when you touch it? What does it smell like? Or sound like? Let yourself be surprised by what your imagination comes up with. Now, you are invited to do something that may in the beginning feel strange. Imagine breathing in and welcoming this pain ... allowing it to transform itself inside you into a softening, healing quality, which you breathe out. Let your imagination do the work; you don't need to try hard ... allow curiosity and playfulness.

So, for example, if you breathe in darkness, you may breathe out brightness ... if you breathe in black smoke, you may breathe out white or golden light ... if you breathe in a particular colour, you may breathe out a complementary colour, e.g. breathing in red, breathing out green... Or breathing in muddiness, breathing out clarity ... breathing in heaviness, coarseness or harshness, breathing out lightness, smoothness or softness ... breathing in heat, breathing out coolness ... breathing in frost, breathing out thaw ... breathing in stench, breathing out fragrance ... breathing in dissonance, breathing out harmony ... breathing in fatigue, breathing out vitality... You can also inhale a dark emotional atmosphere of anxiety, anger or sadness, and exhale a light emotional atmosphere of comfort, tranquillity or joy.

If you lose the soothing breathing rhythm, noticing whatever shows itself... You may be trying to ward off the unpleasant and may notice the energy of the threat system. Or you may be striving for results and recognise the drive system. Acknowledge your experience kindly and allow the calming breath to return before you move on with the imagery practice. If you notice a lot of resistance you can either choose something less painful or practise with the resistance itself. You might experiment with visualising the resistance in front of you... Imagining its qualities, which you breathe in, changing into softening qualities that you breathe out.

You can expand compassionate breathing by adding mindful movements. Stretch out your arms and hands towards the pain in front of you. With every in-breath you move your hands in a receiving gesture towards your heart, with every out-breath you extend your arms and hands in a giving gesture. So, you connect these movements with every breath cycle, while you imagine breathing in what hurts and breathing out what heals... Alternate between practising with and without the movements as you wish.

Kindly explore the effects of this practice, whether pleasant or unpleasant. How does it affect you? There are no wrong experiences. Kindly adapt the practice to your needs. If you feel the space, you may explore another difficulty in a similar way. Continue for as long as you wish.

Building resilience

At first sight, the practice of Compassionate Breathing may seem odd as it goes entirely against the grain of our basic instincts. Surely, you would want to breathe in what you want and breathe out what you don't want? It can be seen as a psychological flu jab, however. Your physical immune system can grow stronger by having to deal with germs or toxins that enter the body in small, manageable amounts. This is how vaccinations work. Likewise, your emotional resilience can grow when you allow what hurts to enter your heart. Of course, it is also important to do this in manageable dosages, allowing time for the healing response to emerge.

By taking in something difficult while calming the threat system and giving away something desirable while calming the drive system, you learn to engage with suffering in a non-selfish way and shift from nourishing an 'ego'-system to nourishing an 'eco'-system.[6] The practice can help to dissolve these strong identifications with pain and be generous in offering healing. It opens our hearts to suffering, whoever is the sufferer.

※ COMPASSIONATE BREATHING: OTHERS

As with Kindness Meditation, it is possible to practise Compassionate Breathing with different categories of other persons or beings, following a similar sequence. Always start from mindful presence and a soothing breathing rhythm and return to it whenever you notice tension or distraction.

Start with a benefactor or with someone who is dear to you. Visualise the person in your mind's eye and reflect on what kind of suffering may play a role in his or her life. Then connect with this pain, sorrow or difficulty and imagine the qualities it may have. It may be that a visual or tangible sense is prominent, or an emotional atmosphere. Imagine breathing in this person's suffering. Welcome and allow it to enter through all pores of your body and let it change into a healing quality, which you breathe out towards this person. It may be that you imagine breathing in something, dark, hot or sticky and breathing out something light, cool and airy. Or you breathe in something cold and hard and breathe out something warm and soft. Let your imagination do the work and be mindful of whatever arises.

Then you can expand the practice in a similar way to a neutral person, a difficult person, groups of other people or animals, and eventually all beings. Be gentle with yourself. It may feel daunting to breathe in the suffering of the world. It is not about working harder, however. It is not about striving to take in or give away what you cannot manage. It is not a practice in grandiosity but rather in humility. Your imagination is doing the work. Allow your mind and heart to open from the calmness of the body, supported by mindful presence and the ebb and flow of the soothing breath. Imagine a manageable proportion of suffering flowing in with every in-breath, which is transformed and healed with every out-breath. Take a mindful pause and return to self-compassion whenever strong emotions or stress reactions surface. Allow the soothing breathing rhythm to return before you continue. You can experiment with adding taking in and giving out movements of the arms and hands.

With every breath, we are interconnected with all other living beings. Our imagination has no limits and our hearts can be as big as the world.

There is plenty of opportunity to practise Compassionate Breathing in daily life. When you meet suffering in yourself, other people or animals, you may not always know what to do or say. This practice can give a deeper meaning to Rumi's poem 'The Guest House',[7] widely quoted in mindfulness courses. Rumi compares being human to a guest house, warmly welcoming all unexpected visitors, also the ones coming in various shapes of suffering. If you invite them in, they may have a precious message to give you.

You may feel barriers or unbridgeable gaps between yourself and the suffering person or the suffering part in yourself. You may work with clients you feel unable to help, find yourself confronted with sick, demented or dying persons, live near intensive farming, or watch the news and see victims of war, traffic or natural disaster. In such difficult moments, you can practise compassionate breathing informally as another variation of the Three Minute Breathing Space. It can be empowering, even when you feel powerless. You are doing something valuable, however modest. You are mindfully and heartfully present with wholesome intentions.

※ BREATHING SPACE WITH COMPASSIONATE BREATHING

The first two steps are similar to the Breathing Space with Compassion.

1 **Being present with open, kind awareness.**
2 **Allowing a soothing breathing rhythm.**
3 **Breathing in what hurts, breathing out what heals.**

Expanding awareness to the breathing body as a whole, as it is taking in and giving out through all its pores in ongoing exchange between what is inside and outside... Attune to whatever suffering is there right now, whether your own or others'... Allow your imagination to come up with whatever attributes this suffering may have... Take the suffering in with every in-breath and allowing it to transform into a healing quality you breathe out... Continue this for as long as you wish... Resume your daily activities when you feel ready to do so.

※ Calendar: Inner Helper

Notice moments when an inner helper manifests itself, observing the experience with curiosity. You can make notes on the worksheet.

Questions for reflection

- What was the situation?
- How and when did you become aware of the inner helper?
- What did the inner helper say to you?
- What did you notice in your body and emotions?
- What are you noticing now, while reflecting on this experience?
- What could be a kind response?

SUMMARY CHAPTER 5

In this chapter we reflect more deeply on the relational qualities of compassion. We cause a lot of suffering in our relationships by holding on to fixed ideas about ourselves and others. Letting go of over-identifications can widen our horizon. Many practices in this training challenge us to embody a best possible version of ourselves. We practise how our compassionate self can relate to a suffering part in ourselves in compassionate letter writing. We explore how we can deal with difficulties in Kindness Meditation and offer an alternative practice without words: Compassionate Breathing.

SUGGESTIONS FOR PRACTICE

Formal

- Take time to practise compassionate letter writing (p. 75–76).
- Expand the Kindness Meditation with a 'difficult' person. 🔊))
- Practise Compassionate Breathing to Yourself 🔊)) and Others 🔊)). If this practice connects well with you, you can do it more regularly as an alternative to Kindness Meditation.
- Return to practices of previous chapters as required.

Informal

- Regularly practise the Breathing Spaces or the Self-Compassion Mantra. When you encounter suffering in yourself or others, you can also do a Breathing Space with Compassionate Breathing (p. 86).
- Calendar: Inner Helper. 📝

Notes

1. Here we present just a brief summary of psychological insights into the self-concept. For more details and references, see Van den Brink. E. & Koster, F. (2015). *Mindfulness-based compassionate living*. London: Routledge.
2. Referred to as self-as-context and self-as-content, see Hayes, S., Strohsal, K., & Wilson, K. (2012). *Acceptance and commitment therapy: The process and practice of mindful change*. New York: Guilford Press.
3. Salzberg, S. (1995). *Loving-kindness*. Boston: Shambhala.
4. Fredrickson, B. L. (2013). *Love 2.0*. New York: Penguin.
5. Chödrön, P. (2001). *Tonglen: The path of transformation*. Halifax, Canada: Vajradhatu.
6. Crocker, J. & Canevello, A. (2012). Egosystem and ecosystem: Motivational perspectives on caregiving. In S. L. Brown, R. M. Brown & L. A. Penner (eds), *Moving beyond self-interest: Perspectives from evolutionary biology, neuroscience, and the social sciences* (pp. 211–223). New York: Oxford University Press. See also Chapter 7.
7. Barks, C. & Moyne, J. (1997) *The essential Rumi*. San Francisco: Harper.

Chapter 6

Making friends for life

Session six: growing happiness

> May the blossom of compassion grow
> in the fertile earth of kindness,
> sprinkled by the fresh water of sympathetic joy,
> in the cool shade of equanimity.
>
> —Tibetan saying

In this chapter, we will offer further practices to strengthen our sense of common humanity. Although we tend to focus on how other people are different from us, we actually have much more in common than differences. We all wish for happiness and freedom from suffering. We will be spending more time on the qualities of the heart, and how they can extend to all people and sentient beings. Of course, in compassion training we give a lot of space to suffering and how to alleviate it. But it is equally important to savour the joyful moments in life and not just to focus on our burdens.

Kissing joy as it flies

> He who binds to himself a joy
> Does the winged life destroy;
> But he who kisses the joy as it flies
> Lives in eternity's sunrise.
>
> —'Eternity' by William Blake[1]

If you have travelled for miles through barren grounds and rough weather, you will welcome passing through a lush landscape with warm sunshine, natural swimming pools, fragrant flowers and trees with juicy fruits to savour. Similarly, after spending a lot of time exploring inner difficulties, it can be very refreshing to savour the pleasures of sensory joys. Remember that by no fault of our own the design of our brain is more equipped for survival than for happiness. We have seen that our memory is like Velcro for the negative and Teflon for the positive. Taking in the bad is not something you need to work on, it is something that just happens. However, taking in the good is something that needs a bit of practice, at least for most of us.[2] Switching on our drive mode and going out looking for pleasure is not a sustainable way to do this. It is when we can dwell in the soothing system that we can mindfully open ourselves to positive experiences, let them sink in and savour them. Clinging to joy only destroys it, as voiced beautifully in Blake's poem. If we learn to kiss joy as it flies, we can appreciate it as long as it is there. The experience will also stick better in our memory, so we can remember it.

In the first chapter, we introduced the Pleasure Walk, to help us become aware of joyful and nourishing moments as they occur. Here is another practice to help cultivate the quality of joy with the help of your memory and imagination.

※ REVISITING THE GOOD

Sit or lie down comfortably, being mindfully present, allowing the breath to soothe you...

Can you think back to a recent situation when you saw something that filled you with joy? Perhaps you saw the smiling face of a dear one, children playing in a park, the beauty of a flower, a landscape, a sunset, or a work of art. Imagine that you are seeing right now what you saw then... What colours, shapes, details touched you and filled you with joy? ... What is happening now when you re-connect with this experience? What are you noticing in your face and body, what in the region of the heart?

Now, remember a situation where you heard something that filled you with joy. Perhaps the sound of laughter, a singing bird, rolling waves or beautiful music. Imagine you are hearing now what you heard then... Exploring what it was in the sound that struck the chord of joy inside, exploring the details of the experience... What are you noticing now in the body and the heart?

Moving on now, to an experience of smelling something that filled you with joy. Perhaps the smell of food, a lovely perfume or a fragrance in nature. Imagine inhaling deeply and smelling now what you smelled then... How does it affect you, in your nose and the rest of the body?

Then, imagine in detail a situation where the sense of taste was the channel of joy. Imagine tasting now what you tasted then and savouring it on your tongue... What are you noticing in your mouth and in the rest of the body?

Explore also a situation where the sense of touch was the source of joy. It may be that you touched something warm or soft, stroked the hair of a loved one or the fur of your pet. It may be that you were touched by feeling the warmth of sunrays, the cool breeze of the wind, the grains of sand between your toes on the beach. Imagine feeling now what you felt then... What sensations are you noticing on your skin, the rest of the body, the region of the heart?

Similarly, you can explore other joyful experiences revealed to you through the different doors of your five senses, whether through seeing, hearing, smelling, tasting or touching. Also, noting the accompanying bodily sensations, associations, thoughts and feelings.

continued

The five senses you just explored connect us with the outer world. We also distinguish a sixth sense, the mind, with which we can think thoughts and feel emotions. Can you remember a situation where this sense of your inner world was the channel of a joyful experience? Maybe you were struck by a beautiful thought or insight, an experience of 'Ah, now I understand', maybe you were touched by a metaphor, story or poem. Imagine you experience now what you experienced then... What was it that touched you ... and how does it affect you now, when you re-connect with it?

Paradoxically, this exercise can sometimes stir up sadness and grief for what is lost or an aching desire for what is missing. Maybe this can be acknowledged and appreciated too, as part of this exercise that may need a compassionate response.

Spend as much time as you like revisiting the good and exploring the wonderful experience of joy. We can find joy anywhere if we open the doors of our senses and take time to mindfully abide with it in the calmness of the soothing system. Even in the midst of darkness, something can lighten up that fills our hearts with joy. You may close this practice by placing a hand on your heart, appreciating the capacity of the heart to be filled with joy and appreciating yourself for taking time for this practice.

Three doors to happiness

In the first chapter, we distinguished between the transitory good feelings of the drive system and the longer-lasting positive emotions of the soothing system. The paradox of striving for happiness from the drive system is that it often results in unhappiness, with ever more frustrations, disappointments and addictions. The more you reach out for happiness, the more it seems to escape. But are there ways to develop more sustainable happiness? We know from research that happiness does not depend so much on *what* happens to you but more on *how* you relate to it.[3] Rich people are not necessarily happier than poor people. Excessive luxury and possessions may even create unhappiness, while suffering can be a gateway to happiness when it is met with compassion. So, what can we say in general about happiness? In the field of positive psychology at least three areas have been recognised that contribute to happiness:[4]

- *the pleasant life*, enjoying life through the senses
- *the engaged life*, warmly connecting with each other and
- *the meaningful life*, finding purpose and commitment to values

The pleasant life is cultivated by practices such as going for a pleasure walk, nourishing the soothing system and taking in, savouring and revisiting the good, like in the last exercise. The engaged life is nourished by practices that bridge the gap between ourselves and others and deepen our sense of common humanity and interconnection with all beings. Before we say more about the meaningful life, we will delve deeper into the engaged life.

Four Friends for Life

So far, we have given a lot of attention to the practice of *kindness* and *compassion*. Now, we also wish to draw two other qualities of the heart, *sympathetic joy* and *equanimity*, into the spotlight. We refer to these heart qualities as the 'Four Friends for Life'. If we cultivate them by practice, they can indeed become dear companions throughout our lifetime. They are key relational qualities as they help us engage with others and ourselves in a non-selfish way. They shift the focus from the egosystem to the ecosystem, or from 'I-llness' to 'WE-llness'. In Buddhism, they are referred to as the 'Illimitables' or 'Immeasurables'.[5] Their practices have indeed no limits and cultivate a boundless heart embracing all beings – past, present and future, near and far. *No one* is excluded, neither our enemies, nor ourselves. You might be raising an eyebrow at this point and thinking 'is this for average mortals like me'. Well, we are not saying it is always easy, but as we hope to show, it might be simpler than you think.

Travellers make use of instruments like compasses and barometers when they journey through unknown territory under changeable weather conditions. Likewise, our 'inner barometer' (*Figure 6.1*) can help us choose which of the heart qualities to practise in different circumstances. *Kindness* is our all-weather friend and can always be practised, certainly in average conditions. But when kindness meets suffering it becomes *compassion*, and that is what we need when our inner weather is bleak, rainy and cold. Kindness becomes *sympathetic joy* when it meets fair, sunny and warm weather conditions, which we can savour, appreciate and celebrate. We can compare *equanimity* with the firm reliable holder, which gives the barometer stability in extremes of temperature, turbulence and unpredictability. Equanimity brings inner stillness and poise in the midst of chaos.

Each heart quality can be a medicine when we are drawn to their opposites that poison our lives and close our hearts. Kindness is a remedy against hatred, compassion against cruelty, sympathetic joy against envy and equanimity against over-involvement and conceit. The Four Friends

Figure 6.1 The Inner Barometer

help us keep the right balance in our practice and avoid the pitfalls of one-sidedness. For instance, if we notice feeling overburdened by the heaviness of suffering in compassion practice, it can do us good to allow more lightness into the practice with loving kindness or sympathetic joy. If we lose our balance because we are too anxious or too eager, or strong emotions overwhelm us, equanimity may be the friend we need. If we notice boredom or indifference, we may return to compassion or sympathetic joy. Thus, we combine the practice of mindfulness with sensing the right tone of heartfulness, attuned to the given circumstances.

It may be helpful to think of a teacher and how she engages with different children in her class. She wants all her pupils to be happy and to do well, which is embodied in her basic attitude of kindness. She shows her appreciative joy to those children who are successful, using their talents and flourishing. She turns with compassion towards those who have learning difficulties, poor health, problems at home or special needs. There may also be children whose behaviour is challenging and antisocial, who bully others and play truant. Her attitude towards those children is characterised by equanimity. She contains her own emotions as well as theirs, sets limits and stands firm. She does not accept the bad behaviour but nevertheless wishes them well and offers adequate space for them to learn.

Below the four heart qualities are compared with each other.

	Incentive	Motive	Remedy against	Pitfall
Kindness	Awareness of the wish to be well	Promoting wellness	Hatred, ill will	Attachment, becoming overly sentimental
Compassion	Awareness of pain and suffering	Alleviating suffering	Cruelty, Schadenfreude	Pity, grave earnestness
Sympathetic joy	Awareness of prosperity and happiness	Celebrating success and happiness	Envy, jealousy	Hypocrisy, overexcitement
Equanimity	Awareness of imbalance and impermanence	Fostering peace, balance and harmony	Over-involvement, bias, conceit	Indifference, apathy

Now, if you feel you need to dwell in pleasant areas for a bit longer, be kind to yourself and practise more savouring and revisiting the good. If you feel ready to explore another area of suffering that you may not have explored before, we would like to invite you to attempt the next challenge.

Giving peace a chance[6]

> *To forgive is to set a prisoner free,*
> *and to discover the prisoner was you.*
>
> —Anonymous

While engagement is associated with happiness, disengagement comes with suffering and unhappiness. What can you do if the road to connection with yourself or others seems blocked? Are there ways of re-connecting? In the previous chapter, you have already practised relating compassionately to a suffering part in yourself and sending kindness to a difficult person. This is particularly difficult if you cannot accept the wrongdoings of yourself or others. We all hurt each other at times, sometimes deliberately and often unintentionally. We can hate ourselves and others deeply for it, and feel stuck in ill will, resentment and inner harshness. But this only creates more suffering. One of the good things about the new brain is that it enables us to practise forgiveness.

Not surprisingly, many religious and wisdom traditions value the practise of forgiveness highly. Archbishop Tutu has talked about why he needed to find a way to forgive those who committed horrendous crimes under the apartheid regime in South Africa.[7] He had to forgive to prevent his heart being poisoned. Forgiveness is not a luxury but a necessity for keeping our sanity. Forgiveness needs compassion, but perhaps even more equanimity, to help us see harmful deeds in a wider perspective and keep our balance in the midst of strong emotions and harsh judgments.

Modern psychology confirms that forgiveness is a golden road to emotional health.[8] It is not easy, however, and that is why we only introduce it at a later stage in the training. So, you are invited to approach this gently. We offer three exercises, inspired by Tara Brach,[9] in which forgiveness can be explored. Perhaps the best way to appreciate the sensitivity of this work is by simultaneously being the giver and the receiver of a forgiving intention, as in the first exercise. If you feel the space, you can proceed with the other two. First, try the practices in the privacy of your own mind and heart. You can always decide later whether you wish to approach others that are involved and actually ask for or offer forgiveness. Let yourself be guided by the wisdom that is being developed in these exercises. They may offer a way to find more inner peace with the cracks in your relationships, with yourself and with others. And who knows, it might lead to broken relationships being mended in some way.

※ FORGIVING YOURSELF

> It is not the perfect, but the imperfect, who have need of love.
> —Oscar Wilde[10]

We all have done things in our lives we regret and where we experience inner harshness towards ourselves. Are you willing to explore such an area in your life, which you find hard to accept? This requires some courage. We suggest you choose something you feel okay to start with; later, you may feel space to explore something more difficult. You may have done or said something that hurt somebody, or avoided something you should have done. You may have let down a friend, yelled unreasonably at your child, forgotten a birthday card, neglected your pet, or avoided telling the truth to your

continued

partner. You may have been rude or missed a chance to be kind. You may feel shame, guilt or remorse when you think of it.

If you have picked out something, start with pausing mindfully and welcoming a soothing breathing rhythm... Remember, you can return to this basic practice again and again. It may also help to remind yourself of connecting with a compassionate companion or with the practice of embodying compassion, now and any time you find yourself slipping back into harsh self-judgment.

Begin with looking around in this area of harshness, curiously exploring it as an inner landscape. What is there to discover ... how does the body feel, what emotions surface, what thoughts, images, stories cross your mind...? Look at it non-judgmentally, connecting with your intention to alleviate suffering.

While you explore this area of harshness, let a number of questions drop in and see what they touch inside. Do not force any answers. Be with the questions and mindfully notice what reactions and responses arise by themselves.

How did this inner harshness arise and develop? Do you remember where and when you did what you did? What happened? Did you do it on purpose? Was it a conscious decision or an impulse on the spur of a moment? Were you perhaps in threat or drive mode, caught up in a stress reaction or inner pattern? Did you choose the causes from which this behaviour arose? Did you foresee the consequences of what you did? Would you do it again with the wisdom you have now? How many people do you imagine are walking around on this globe who have done something similar in their lives? Is there anything worthwhile you have learned or could learn from it?

Now, this exercise is not about condoning mistakes or unwise behaviour. It is an invitation to make peace with the vulnerable, imperfect person behind this behaviour. Yes, yourself – like most human beings, not quite perfect. Most of us do things we later regret. Often, our wisdom is on vacation. We may lack clarity, feel overburdened or tired. We may follow emotions blindly and act on instinct, out of fear, anger or jealousy. We forget to pause before we act and do not foresee the consequences of our behaviour. What about acknowledging your imperfections and considering making peace with yourself?

Just taste this word on your tongue ... forgiveness. What would it be like to forgive yourself? You can just try it out and say for instance, 'I understand what I did was causing harm. I am willing to learn from this. I see that not forgiving myself is causing further harm. Therefore, I forgive myself.' Can you say this from your heart and receive it? Mindfully observe what happens... There are no wrong experiences here. Maybe it softens the harshness inside, maybe not. If the words can be received, carry on by gently repeating 'I forgive myself'...

If you feel resistance, forgiveness might not be the connecting word you need to hear just now. Maybe other words, phrases or reflections connect better... What about forgivingness, the intention to forgive. 'May I be willing to forgive myself at some stage...', or 'I wish myself reconciliation ... understanding ... comfort ... peace...', or 'May I learn from my mistakes'... If somebody else suffered from what you did, a wish in the we-form may connect well. 'May we make peace' or 'May we live in harmony'... The words may be supported by a gentle smile on your face or a hand on your heart.

Sometimes, there are no fitting words. Then you may wish to practise compassionate breathing, which does not need words. Imagine placing the harshness, the pain or your resistance in front of you, breathing it in and allowing it to transform into a softening energy, which you breathe out. And of course, if you don't feel much space around the theme you have explored, you may forgive yourself for this and appreciate you at least made a start with this difficult work.

The following lines by the Spanish poet Antonio Machado[11] may offer inspiration.

Last night as I was sleeping,
I dreamt – blessed illusion! –
there was a beehive
in my heart.
And the golden bees
were making
white wax and sweet honey
from my old bitterness.

Questions for reflection

- What area of inner harshness did you explore?
- What did you notice in your body, emotions and thoughts?
- How did this area of inner harshness develop?
- Did you do it on purpose?
- Could you foresee the consequences at the time?
- What was it like to offer yourself forgiveness?
- Was there a word, wish, image or gesture having a softening effect?
- What are you noticing now, while reflecting on this exercise?
- What could be a kind wish to yourself now?

※ ASKING FORGIVENESS

In this exercise, you can explore your willingness to ask forgiveness from a person you have hurt, harmed or wronged in any way. In real life this can be very hard. 'Sorry seems to be the hardest word' has become a classic song.[12] But you do not need to feel ready to ask forgiveness in real life yet. You can start doing this in your imagination. Whether the person concerned is inclined to grant forgiveness is not important for this practice. All you are doing is opening a way to reconciliation with this person from your side. Of course, it is hard to ask forgiveness if you are unable to forgive yourself. So, if you find this is the case, then return to the previous practice.

Bring the situation to mind in which you hurt the other person. Imagine the situation in as much detail as your memory allows and particularly focussing on the pain or disappointment you may have caused the other person. Imagining you are feeling what he or she felt... Now see if you feel space to forgive yourself first. Then, imagine looking this other person in the eyes. You can softly whisper their name, followed by words like: 'I understand I caused you pain and feel sorry for what I did... I cannot change the past but I value our relationship and wish we may live in harmony, now and in the future... May you, at some stage, forgive me... May we live in peace...'

continued

> *Instead of working with words, you can practise compassionate breathing. Imagine breathing in the pain you have caused the other person, allowing it to transform in your heart into a healing, consoling or comforting quality that you breathe out towards that person.*

※ FORGIVING OTHERS

> Vengeance is a lazy form of grief.
> —Unknown source

Just as you have hurt others in your life, there are probably others who have hurt you. If your heart has hardened towards them, this is a third area to explore. Can you contemplate forgiveness towards somebody who has caused you pain and suffering? Approach this area only when you have enough clarity of mind and space in your heart to do so. Do not begin with the most difficult person. Remember that forgiving others is not about condoning their behaviour. It is about stopping unnecessary suffering. You have suffered already from the deed itself and will continue to suffer if you poison yourself with destructive emotions, like hate, resentment and grudge. You may feel the other person does not deserve forgiveness, but what about you? Do you deserve peace? So, would you give peace a chance?

Forgiving others starts with self-compassion, by mindfully acknowledging your pain and reactive emotions and all the judgments and stories your mind builds around it. If you can hold your suffering and reactivity with compassion, then you may feel ready to open your heart to the person who hurt you and see behind their behaviour. Can you see in this person a vulnerable human being, like yourself, who longs for happiness and freedom from suffering? He or she may not have had much choice in the conditions that led up to the behaviour that hurt you and may not have seen the consequences of what they did. Even if there was the intention to harm you, this person has probably been treated badly by others.

Imagine this person at a safe distance and see if you can make a step towards forgiveness. You may look into the other person's eyes, say their name and reflect as follows:

> *I feel the pain and my reactions to what you did. I do not find this easy, but I wish to do what I can to relieve the suffering that resulted from what you did, both in me and in you. We cannot change the past, but we can hope for a better future. We all have our imperfections and the many conditions that shaped our lives were not our choice. What you did was not right, but I forgive you as a human being...*

You can then gently repeat a kind wish that softens your heart towards this person, in a 'you' or in a 'we' phrase, e.g. 'May wisdom grow out of our past mistakes... May we be free from suffering... May we live in peace...'

Mindfully explore the effects of this practice. Be true to yourself and adjust the words if you find forgiving is too difficult for now. Return to self-compassion as much as you need. Wishes like 'May I be open to the intention to forgive...' or 'May I be open for reconciliation...' might be more feasible. Compassionately breathing your own pain or the pain of the other person and breathing out a healing energy, can be an alternative.

Exploring painful areas in ourselves can stir up old grief and sadness but it can also make us more aware of what really matters to us. In forgiveness work a sense of deep gratitude can fill our hearts if we feel truly forgiven or if we can sincerely forgive another person and appreciate what we have learned from the pain and suffering.

Gratitude: the memory of the heart[13]

Receiving something we appreciate, can fill us with joy or relief. *Gratitude* is a deep appreciation of what is given to us. We value the gift and treasure it in our hearts, so it can travel with us wherever we go. You may have noticed in the exercise Revisiting the Good that joy and gratitude are closely connected. But finding relief from pain or making peace with something troublesome, can also be received with gratitude.

Gratitude connects us with the meaningful life. You can rationally think about life's purpose and consult numerous scholars and books. But, quite likely, the question 'What is the purpose of *your* life?' remains unanswered. Feeling grateful connects us with what matters in life. We do not need to *think* of life's meaning anymore. We *feel* it, and therefore we *know* it.

Being mindfully aware of what fills us with gratitude is a wholesome practice. Research has confirmed that reflecting regularly on what you feel grateful for makes you feel happier and healthier.[14] For many religious people saying a prayer of thanks is part of their daily rituals. Also, non-religious people can cultivate a regular gratitude practice. In either case, the practice will be more powerful if you do it mindfully. The following exercise could be a good start.

※ GRATITUDE

Find yourself a comfortable position, allowing for mindful presence and a soothing breath. Then, invite things to come up for which you feel grateful or appreciative. These may be circumstances, events, people, animals, nature ... memories of what you experienced recently or longer ago... They may also concern personal qualities and talents you feel contented with, things you have learned, developed and shared... Hold the things that fill you with gratitude one by one in your awareness... Ask yourself each time 'What is it here that strikes the gratitude chord in me? What do I notice in my body, my heart and mind? What do I notice now I reflect on it?'

So, you can continue exploring the inner landscape of gratitude. If you would like to take notes, you can use the worksheet.

Now, it is not easy to find meaning in life, let alone feel grateful, if bad things happen to us. What purpose can be found in war and disaster, in trauma, loss, illness and death? Perhaps one of the greatest capacities of human beings is that meaning can be found in even the worst conditions. The best-loved fairy tales and epic stories are often about finding hidden treasures and light coming out of darkness. Maybe you have experienced yourself how inner strength and resilience can grow in adversity. The next exercise is named after the proverb 'Every cloud has a silver lining'. In a training session, we usually ask participants to do this in pairs.

※ THE SILVER LINING

It is the headwind which causes the kite to rise.

—Chinese saying

Begin as usual, with mindfulness and a soothing breathing rhythm. Now gently connect with a difficult period in your life. Choose something you feel you can reflect on. Take your time to look at this dark cloud in your personal history. Then begin to explore if you can also see a silver lining. Has anything good come out of this difficult experience? Have you perhaps learned something from it that you may not have learned otherwise? Similarly, you can reflect on other dark periods in your life and focus on their silver linings.

Now, think of an area of darkness in your current life, an area of suffering or a dilemma you find yourself stuck with. What silver lining do you wish yourself to emerge round this dark cloud you are facing now? What do you wish you will have learned from it, when you look back on it later? Or another metaphor: what lotus flower do you hope will grow out of this mud? Similarly, you can think of other muddy areas in your life, contemplating the lotus flowers you would wish to grow out of them.

If you do this exercise on your own, you may end with kind wishes, connected to the silver linings or lotus flowers that came up, gently repeating them on the rhythm of the soothing breath. If you do this exercise in pairs, you can tell the other person about the good that has come out of a difficulty in the past. One person speaks mindfully, the other listens mindfully without saying anything. Then you change roles. Similarly, you can take turns to share the good you wish to come out of a current difficulty in your life. Later, you can reflect in mindful dialogue. What was it like to be the speaker and silently being listened to? What was it like to be the listener and receive what the speaker said? What resonated in your own heart?

The next exercise may cast more light on the meaningful life. It is an invitation to reflect on the *values* that touch your heart and give your life a sense of purpose and direction. A core value is like a lighthouse in the distance, keeping you on track. In darkness and rough weather, sailors may hardly see a thing, but they can still see the lighthouse in the distance. Values are not like goals you can simply reach. Achievable goals may be derived from them, but values themselves are never accomplished and require ongoing commitment. Examples of core values are friendship, love, justice, peace, care for nature, health and spirituality.

※ YOUR VALUES

> He who has a 'why' to live can bear almost any 'how'.
> —Friedrich Nietzsche[15]

Start with mindful pausing and allowing relaxation to enter the body... Now reflect on what you truly value. What would you wish your life to stand for? It may help to imagine how you would wish to look back on your life in ten or 20 years, or when your end is near... Or, you can take it yet another step further. Imagine your dear ones are gathered at your funeral. What would you like them to say about you and your life? How would you like them to remember you? What words would be fitting as an epitaph? Take your time to answer these questions and the ones below. If no answers come, allow the questions to sink in and touch whatever lets itself be touched.

- *What are your values? What do you wish your life to stand for?*
- *How do you give expression to these values in your daily life?*
- *What stands in the way of expressing your values?*
- *What could support you in expressing your values?*
- *What could be a kind wish for yourself?*

You can make notes on the worksheet if you like.

Committing your life to your values can fill it with meaning, vitality and happiness. So, the reward of following your heart does not lie in the future, but is experienced here and now. Of course, you will also meet painful hurdles on the way, but this does not make your values any less worthwhile. On the contrary, it hurts because they are so valuable. As Acceptance and Commitment therapists say, in your pain you meet your values; in your values you meet your pain.[16] Science increasingly confirms what we knew all along from our wisdom traditions, that prosocial values connect most strongly with happiness.[17]

What would be more fitting than to conclude this chapter with a further expansion of the Kindness Meditation, this time to all beings?

※ KINDNESS MEDITATION: GROUPS AND ALL BEINGS

Choose a comfortable position, sitting or lying. Begin as always with the first two steps of the Breathing Space with Kindness. Start with repeating a kind wish that connects well with yourself right now.

Then choose a group you belong to, for instance your family, your colleagues at work, your sports club, your meditation group, the people in your street, your village, town, country. What would be a kind wish for this group? Gently repeat the wish on the rhythm of the soothing breath. 'May we feel safe ... healthy ... happy ... at ease...' Or any other wish you feel connects well with the group you have in mind. Gently

continued

repeat the wish on the rhythm of the breath or independently from it... Expanding to other groups you belong to.

Moving on to other groups. Perhaps groups that were in the news or that you heard about from others. People in different countries and different parts of the world, men, women, children, elderly, groups of animals. There is no need to strive at including everyone. If you feel overwhelmed, powerless or insignificant, you can always return to self-compassion, before you continue with a new group. If you find it difficult to connect with a group you can zoom in on the face of one individual in this group whom you know from TV or a photograph. Imagine your eyes meet and realise this human being wishes for happiness and freedom from suffering, just like yourself. Send kindness or compassion to this person... Then zoom out again and send kindness to the whole group. 'May you be free from suffering ... feel at ease ... find peace and harmony.'

If there is doubt whether your wishing will have any effect whatsoever, notice your thoughts and feelings. Whether others will be affected can remain an open question; you may notice effects in yourself. There are no wrong experiences, mindfully acknowledging what shows itself, feeling free to send kindness to yourself until you feel space to return to groups again.

You can conclude the practice with kindness to all beings, humans, animals, plants and trees, wherever in the universe, whether living in the past, present or future. The practice is boundless, because our imaginative minds and tender hearts are boundless. 'May all beings feel safe ... healthy ... happy ... at ease... May all beings live in peace with themselves and each other.'

※ Calendar: Receiving Compassion

During the coming week you can explore situations in which you receive kindness or compassion from others. You can take notes on what you observe in body, thoughts and feelings.

Questions for reflection

- What was the situation?
- How did you become aware of receiving compassion?
- What physical sensations did you notice?
- What thoughts and emotions did you notice?
- What are you noticing now, while reflecting on this experience?

SUMMARY CHAPTER 6

In this chapter we reflect on the boundless qualities of the heart, which we refer to as The Four Friends for Life: kindness, compassion, sympathetic joy and equanimity. We can deepen our practice by cultivating these four in the right balance. We explore how happiness can be nourished by living a joyful, engaged and meaningful life. We also introduce the practice of forgiveness, as a way of healing cracks in our relationships, with ourselves and with others.

SUGGESTIONS FOR PRACTICE

Formal

- Practise Revisiting the Good. ◀))
- Explore one or more of the three areas of Forgiveness: Forgiving Yourself ◀)) 🗒, Asking Forgiveness ◀)) and Forgiving Others ◀)).
- Expand the Kindness Meditation with groups and all beings. ◀))
- Reflect on Gratitude 🗒, The Silver Lining and Your Values 🗒.
- Return to the practices of previous chapters as required.

Informal

- Regularly practise the Breathing Spaces or Self-Compassion Mantra.
- Calendar: Receiving Compassion. 🗒

Silent session

To the mind that is still,
the whole universe surrenders.

—Lao Tzu

Between the sixth and seventh session in the course we offer an extra session of guided meditations and silent practice. It is usually referred to as a silent session because participants are not exchanging experiences of their practice as in other sessions. Also, in the refreshment break they do not talk. For practical reasons, this session may have the same length as other sessions, but we recommend giving it more time. A half day or full day, as is offered in many mindfulness courses, is ideal. If you are following a group training, the teacher will decide on the content. We usually offer practices that cultivate the good and do not focus on the exercises that explore specific difficulties. We guide various imagery practices intertwined with the complete sequence of kindness meditations, alternating between sitting, lying, walking and mindful movement. If you use this book as a self-help guide you may wish to offer yourself a mini retreat or arrange one with friends. Below, an example is given of a programme for half a day (4 hours).

Example of a silent session programme

- Beginning: Welcome, intentions, poem (10 minutes)
- Sitting: Kindness to Self/Benefactor/Dear Person (20 minutes)
- Mindful Movement (15 minutes)
- Walking: Kindness to Self/Neutral Person (15 minutes)

continued

- Lying: Imagery practice Safe Place/Compassionate Companion/Embodying Compassion (25 minutes)
- Sitting: Kindness to Self/'Difficult' Person, alternated with Compassionate Breathing (25 minutes)
- Mindful Savouring (break held in silence with tea/coffee/light food), followed by Pleasure Walk (30 minutes)
- Sitting: Revisiting the Good (20 minutes)
- Lying: Kindness to the Body or An Appreciative Body Scan ◀)) (20 minutes)
- Sitting: Imagery practice, e.g. the Horse Whisperer ◀)) or the River of Life ◀)) (25 minutes)
- Mindful Movement (10 minutes)
- Sitting: Kindness to Groups and All Beings (15 minutes)
- Ending: Brief sharing, transition to everyday life (10 minutes)

Do not hesitate to adjust the programme according to your needs and alternate the compassion practices with silent unguided practice. You can use some of the audios. A simpler version of the Kindness Meditation involving all categories from Yourself to All Beings is available as an audio download ◀)). You can also practise guiding yourself. Or you can take it in turns when you practise with others. An electronic timer and bell might be handy. At the end it is recommended to allow some time for reflection and sharing with other participants, taking care to ensure a gradual transition back into everyday life.

Here are two examples of guided exercises we may offer during a silent practice session. The first one is an alternative version of a well-known practice from the mindfulness course.

※ AN APPRECIATIVE BODY SCAN

In this exercise, you are invited to lie down in a quiet place, taking care that your body is comfortable, warm and well supported. If you cannot lie down for long, adjust your position as you wish, for example sitting or half-sitting.

This exercise invites you to travel mindfully through every part of the body just as in the practice of the bodyscan from the mindfulness course. This time, however, with specific attention to how to cultivate a deeper appreciation of the body.

Start with mindfully becoming aware of the body as it is right now, sensing the surface on which it rests and the subtle sensations of air and textures that envelop it ... surrendering to the force of gravity, letting all the tension go that you do not need to hold on to ... allowing the body to be soothed and softened by the breath... As if all bodily parts are free to be released from their joints, trusting the body will keep itself together, without you having to put any effort into it... Appreciate the body as your faithful companion, however imperfect it may be, however vulnerable to injury, illness and aging ... releasing it from having to do anything, allowing it to rest in the cradle of your kind and caring awareness and letting it enjoy the peace and stillness of simply being as it is...

Then bring your attention to the feet, welcoming them in your awareness ... noticing any sensations of temperature or touch, lightness or heaviness, energy or vibration... Just realise how these feet have carried your body to so many places, from the first day you could walk until now... What kind wish could you have for your feet? You can gently work with the soothing breath, bringing your attention closer on the in-breath, sensing how your feet feel and allowing a fitting kind or compassionate wish to flow towards them on the out-breath... For example, 'May you be strong' or 'May you feel at ease'... As if they are personal friends, treating them with the best intentions ... appreciating your feet for all their service and mindfully noticing how they receive this kindness and appreciation.

Then travel on through your ankles, lower legs, knees, upper legs and hips ... realising these parts enable you to walk, hike, bike, play sports, dance ... sensing and appreciating every part, muscle group and joint... Expand your awareness to your entire legs and allowing waves of kindness and gratitude to flow towards them ... and noticing how this is received.

Likewise sensing your pelvis and spine, appreciating their strength and flexibility for keeping you balanced and upright ... offering these parts kindness and gratitude.

Then, travel on through your abdomen and chest ... connecting mindfully with the areas where your inner organs reside, taking time to realise how they help you function 24 hours a day, from the day you came into existence until now... The wonders of your digestive system, extracting nutrition from your food, disposing of waste ... your kidneys, managing the balance of minerals and fluids ... your lungs, inhaling and exhaling the air in perpetual exchange with other living beings ... your heart and blood vessels, circulating the blood that nourishes and detoxifies every part and organ in the body ... gently sensing and appreciating all these bodily parts ... offering them kindness and gratitude ... and noticing how this is received.

Even when functions are faltering or lost, you may appreciate these parts of your body for what they made possible in your life and send them gratitude for how they served you and what they mean to you right now. These parts can be an invitation to deepen your compassion practice.

Travel on through your upper limbs, sensing and appreciating your shoulders, arms, hands and fingers, which enable you to move, carry things, use instruments, make gestures, touch and feel, play music, write and type ... offering them kindness and gratitude with every breath ... noticing how the giving and receiving affects you.

Continue with sensing and appreciating your neck and throat ... your mouth, tongue and jaws, enabling you to taste, eat, speak ... your facial muscles, enabling you to express a range of emotional language ... your nose, enabling you to breathe and smell ... your eyes making it possible to see ... your ears enabling you to hear ... allowing gratitude to enter all these areas ... sensing and appreciating the inside of your head, where your brains are at home, continuously processing information coming in and going out, communicating with other parts of the body through the nervous system, through spinal cord and countless nerves.

Finally, widen your awareness to your entire body... Allow kindness to flow through every cell of it... If you like, carried by the rhythm of the breath, imagining a wave of appreciation and gratitude flowing with every breath from the crown of your head to the tip of your toes and back again ... or from the centre of the body to the surface of your skin and back again ... allowing the body to rest in a healing bath of kindness, compassion, appreciation and gratitude.

Take your time to end this exercise... You may gently wriggle your fingers and toes and move the body in a way it wants to be moved... You may wish to do some mindful stretches before you get up and resume your daily activities.

A silent session can be a good opportunity to introduce helpful metaphors, poems or stories to aid the practice. Metaphors that are often used in the mindfulness courses are the mountain for sitting meditation and the lake for lying down meditation. People may relate differently to different metaphors. They may touch us on different levels of our being. Allow metaphors to do their work but if nothing much happens, that is fine too.

The following story offers another metaphor, inspired by a novel by Nicholas Evans.[18] For didactic reasons, we have created a simplified version in our own words, leaving out many details and enhancing the metaphor by some additions.

※ THE HORSE WHISPERER

Take your time to settle into a comfortable sitting position, being present to the experience of the moment and allowing the breath to find its soothing rhythm... Now, mindfully acknowledge what arises while you listen to the following story:

A young teenage girl loves to spend as much time as she can with her horse. One day, she rides her horse in the snow. The weather conditions are turning bad. She loses control over her horse and they slip. They slide down a hill towards the road and are hit by a big truck. They both survive, but their lives will never be the same. The girl, who lives with her mother, is left walking with a limp. She experiences dark moods. She has lost her best and most beloved friend who has turned into an anxious, irritable and restless animal. The horse does not trust humans anymore and is unmanageable, so it is kept in the stable. The mother tries everything to cheer her daughter up and understands that the only way to help her daughter is to heal the relationship with her horse. She tries hard to find a cure.

Her search eventually leads to a man who is said to have specials skills with traumatised horses. He lives far away in a remote part of the country. They drive hundreds of miles with the horse in a van. Then they meet a remarkable man who says very little. He points out they can stay at his ranch for as long as they need, but they must leave the horse to him. To their surprise, he brings the animal to a vast open field where he releases it, so it can roam freely. The horse runs and runs until they can hardly see it anymore. The mother and daughter already strongly doubt their decision to trust this man, but he seems confident in what he is doing.

They witness how he returns daily to the field, where he stands or sits motionlessly on the same spot, looking in the direction of the horse. They see how the animal slowly comes closer, a bit more every day. The man does not reach out; he just sits quietly, watching the horse attentively. He just seems to softly whisper words or sounds in the direction of the horse from time to time. They cannot hear what he whispers, but it seems to encourage the horse to come a bit closer every day. One day, it is almost within touching distance. But when the man lifts his arm to stroke it, the horse is startled and runs off into the distance again.

The whole process starts anew. The man stays on his spot, just watching attentively and whispering softly, letting the horse come nearer at its own pace. The man waits with endless patience, whispering sounds or words that are only meant for the horse to hear. When it is again near enough for the man to touch it, he remains still until the horse rests its head on the man's shoulder. He lets the horse examine him and very carefully he begins to stroke the horse's head and neck, who now lets him do so.

From then on, the horse gains trust and lets itself be approached by the man. Finally, it allows itself to be saddled, so the man can ride it. And then the girl, who now understands why this man is called the Horse Whisperer, learns to reconnect with the horse as well, with patience and kindness. The girl is thrilled when the horse accepts her for a ride again and their friendship is restored.

Now, this story may inspire you how to sit with whatever is in your experience, like a horse whisperer, being silently present with what shows itself, whether thoughts, feelings or other sensations... As if your experiences are like horses in a boundless field, where they can roam freely. Sometimes, they may come on their own, sometimes they may arrive in busy herds... sometimes quietly, sometimes wildly... You do not have to reach out to capture them, you do not have to back off from them... You are just patiently waiting for them to approach you ... kindly acknowledging them, grounded in mindful presence ... if you like by gently whispering words of kindness... No controlling, no pushing or pulling ... just letting yourself be touched by what you experience ... and gently touching your experience without disturbing it ... mindfully, 'kindfully' and with equanimity...

Particularly when a hurt, shy or mistrustful part in you presents itself, it can be helpful to remind yourself of the wisdom and the patience of the horse whisperer. Giving this vulnerable part space in the boundless field of your awareness... Sitting firmly on the ground of your being ... offering unconditional mindful attention ... whispering words of kindness this vulnerable part needs to hear ... waiting for it to come nearer by itself ... letting your mind and heart be touched by it ... and touching it in return in a way it allows you to touch it, without forcing anything ... caring for it without scaring it...

The above story may be helpful to understand how the attitude of compassion can shift towards equanimity and inspire you to deal with the hurt parts in you, the parts that have difficulty receiving kindness and react with backdraft. If you try to force your kindness on them, you will only scare those parts off. Practising with the patience of a horse whisperer may eventually lead to healing your relationship with them.

Notes

1.   William Blake (1994). *Poems*. London: Everyman's Library.
2.   Hanson, R. (2013). *Hardwiring happiness*. New York: Harmony.
3.   Lyubomirsky, S. (2007). *The how of happiness: A practical guide to getting the life you want*. London: Sphere.
4.   Seligman, M. (2002). *Authentic happiness: Using the new positive psychology to realize your potential for lasting fulfillment*. New York: Free Press.
5.   Feldman, C. (2017). *Boundless heart: The Buddha's path of kindness, compassion, joy, and equanimity*. Boulder, CO: Shambhala; Wallace, B. A. (2010). *The four immeasurables: Practices to open the heart*. Boston, MA: Shambala.

6. Paraphrasing the title of the song 'Give peace a chance' written by John Lennon, released in 1969.

7. Tutu, D. (2009). *No future without forgiveness*. New York: The Doubleday Religious Publishing Group.

8. Hall, J. H., & Fincham, F. D. (2005). Self-forgiveness: The stepchild of forgiveness research. *Journal of Social and Clinical Psychology, 24,* 621–637; Toussaint, L., & Friedman, P. (2008). Forgiveness, gratitude, and well-being: The mediating role of affect and beliefs. *Journal of Happiness Studies, 10,* 635–654.

9. Brach, T. (2004). *Radical acceptance*. New York: Bantam.

10. Wilde, O. (1899). *An ideal husband*. London: Leonard Smithers.

11. Excerpt poem 'Anoche cuando dormía' (free translation) from: Machado, A. (1907). *Soledades, galerias y otros poemas*. Madrid: Libreria Pueyo.

12. Song written by Elton John and Bernie Taupin, released in 1976.

13. From a French proverb.

14. Emmons, R. A., & McCullough, M. E. (2003). Counting blessings versus burdens: An experimental investigation of gratitude and subjective well-being in daily life. *Journal of Personality and Social Psychology, 84,* 377–389.

15. From: Twilight of the Idols (1889).

16. Hayes, S., Strohsal, K., & Wilson, K. (2012). *Acceptance and commitment therapy: The process and practice of mindful change*. New York: Guilford Press.

17. Klein, S. (2014). *Survival of the nicest: How altruism made us human and why it pays to get along*. New York: The Experiment; Ricard, M. (2015). *Altruism*. London: Atlantic.

18. Evans, N. (1995). *The horse whisperer*. New York: Delacorte Press.

Chapter 7

Heartful mind, mindful heart

Session seven: weaving wisdom and compassion into daily life

> *Integrity is doing the right thing, even when no one is watching.*
>
> —Anonymous

Approaching the end of the course, we shall now focus more on how to link the practices to the heart and soul of daily life. There would be little point in doing lots of formal practices, if they did not spill out into our daily activities in many informal ways. The following exercise invites you to look closer at an average day of your life.

※ A DAY IN YOUR LIFE

Give yourself a few minutes to pause mindfully, giving space to a soothing breathing rhythm. Then divide a blank sheet of paper into three columns, the left column being wide, and the central and right ones narrower. You can also download the worksheet for this. List the daily activities of an average day in your life in the wide left column, from waking up to going to bed. Mark in the column on the far right to what extent you do that activity out of care for yourself. You can score this with a number from 1 to 5, where 1 = not at all, and 5 = very much so, or a number in between. Do not give it a lot of thinking but follow your first inclination. Once you are ready you can fold the column backwards so you do not see it anymore. Then, mark in the middle column to what extent you do that activity out of care for one or more other persons, animals or other living creatures. Score this in the same way: 1 = not at all; 5 = very much so.

When you have completed this, open the sheet again and just look at your list, mindfully noticing any reactions, giving yourself time to reflect on a number of questions.

– Are scores evenly divided in both columns? Do scores on self-care and care for others for a specific activity match or do they differ?

continued

> - *How do you feel about the balance beween self-care and care for others? Contented, neutral, or uneasy?*
> - *In session 7 of the mindfulness training, participants are usually asked to explore how their daily activities drain or supply energy. How do activities scoring high or low on self-care and care for others, relate to your energy and stress levels? Do they make you feel tired, excited, or refreshed?*
> - *Remember the three emotion regulation systems are also called motivation systems. Do you recognise the predominance of the threat, drive or soothing systems when you perform certain activities? Or are there perhaps particular stress reactions or inner patterns prevailing?*
> - *Is there perhaps an inner critic, an inner slave driver or an inner helper at your side while you do these activities?*
> - *What about your deeper motivations? Are activities based on me-first, you-first or we-together motivations? Are they in line with your core values?*
> - *If you feel you could bring more kindness and compassion into your daily life, would it mean doing more or doing less of specific activities?*
> - *If it is difficult to change 'what' you do, it is perhaps possible to look at 'how' you do it. What could be helpful intentions, motivations and attitudes when you are involved with an activity?*

If you find it hard to choose an average day in your life, you can assess one or two days when you do quite different activities. Revisit the above questions as often as you wish during the following week.

Your first assessment may be seen in a different light when you mindfully reflect on it. Below, you can read some examples of participants reflecting upon their daily activities. We have given them fictitious names.

Sarah takes the dog out before going to work, when she is usually pressed for time. She has scored high on care for the dog and low on care for herself. However, on reflecting, she comes to realise that thanks to her dog she is offered a wonderful chance to start the day with a mindful pleasure walk, which is also kind and caring to herself. This may also set the tone for bringing more mindfulness and kindness to the rest of the day. It does not need to cost her extra time, just a switch in motivation.

Mark cycles to work instead of taking the car. He scores this high on self-care because it keeps him fit. He scores it nil on care for others. However, his reflections make him realise his fitness also serves others. It makes him arrive at work in better spirits, so he is better company for his colleagues and his clients. Besides, cycling is a way of being kind to the environment. So, on second thoughts, Mark realises the activity is not selfish at all. He is pleased to bring his motivation for cycling in line with what he values, namely connecting with people and caring for the planet.

Rita is a secretary who works many extra hours to compensate for her colleagues being off sick. She scores this high on care for others and low on self-care. She ponders on her deeper motivation for why she does this. She feels a strong need to be loyal to others and please her boss (you-first motivation). She also hopes for a better position and more pay (me-first motivation). But her efforts cause her to feel exhausted at the end of the day. She risks being next in line to suffer burnout. Then, not only she, but also her company and family, will suffer. If she restores a better balance by allowing more rest and space to the soothing system, she not only cares better for herself, but in the end by doing this she also cares for her family, her boss, the company and its customers (we-together motivation). Rita decides to work less overtime and explain to her boss that taking good care of her health is ultimately better for all.

Chris watches his favourite TV series for one or two hours in the evening before he goes to bed. He scores this activity high on self-care and also on care for others, because he simultaneously chats with his friends on social media. On reflecting, he realises this combination raises his stress-level and makes it difficult to fall asleep once he gets to his bed. He recognises being in drive mode for information from the TV and his friends. But the threat mode is also around as he fears losing their friendship if he does not join in. He decides not to watch TV and follow social media at the same time anymore and regularly check in with his breathing, to allow it to find a soothing rhythm. He will let his friends know when he is available for chatting.

Gwen is a single parent, finding it a challenge to put her two young children to bed after a busy day. They are always noisy and boisterous, just when she is desperate for some peace. She often loses her temper with them and feels guilty afterwards. She has scored this activity low on both sides and cries when asked how this relates to what she really values in life. No doubt, her children are Number One and ending the day in harmony would be so much better. She decides to give them more time, inviting them to share about their day and reading them a story. This way, putting the kids to bed may be nourishing for all.

Draining or sustaining

Doing things in threat or drive modes may sometimes be necessary. However, this drains your batteries very quickly, particularly if these are not recharged by the energy-restoring soothing system. Even activities scoring high on self-care may on closer examination not be so caring at all, particularly if you perform them under the pressure to achieve or avoid unpleasant experiences. It can make a lot of difference whether you do your running exercise because you anxiously want to minimise health risk (threat system), because you are eager to excel in sports (drive system), or because you enjoy and savour being outdoors (soothing system). Activities involving helping others may also drain your energy if they derive from you-first motivation or compulsory tend-and-befriend reactions while you ignore your own needs. If they come from a me-first motivation, you may be driven by a need for being liked and rewarded or by a fear of being ignored or rejected. Helping others from a we-together motivation may bring your threat, drive and soothing systems into a healthier balance, giving you energy and fulfilment.

Egosystem or ecosystem

Nowadays, grave concerns about the condition of our planet regularly reach the headlines. Many people understandably worry about the effects of pollution, global warming and depletion of resources. Sustainability is increasingly becoming a key-issue for policymakers. It is a challenge to shift from policies that drain towards policies that sustain our planet, its inhabitants and future generations.

There is an African saying 'alone we may go faster, together we can come further'. For sustainable health and happiness, we must look at long-term benefits for many rather than short-term profits for few. Sustainability requires a shift in focus from 'me' to 'we'. Ultimately, every being – past, present, future – belongs to the 'we' of the larger whole of the world we are all part of.

It has been shown that couple relationships flourish better and last longer if partners care about the ecosystem of their relationship and their shared needs, rather than the individual needs of their egosystems.[1] This may very likely be true for any relationship. With every breath, we are in exchange with other living beings. If we look at ourselves and others as interconnected and interdependent beings, we may find that caring for ourselves and others are not so different. If we care wisely and compassionately for ourselves, everyone we relate to can benefit. If we care wisely and compassionately for others, we benefit ourselves.

If we want to change the world, there is no better place to start than with ourselves. However, not with ourselves as egosystems but as part of larger ecosystems. Egosystems are constantly in need of defence against other egosytems. As we discussed in Chapter 5, the more rigidly we identify with them the more they get in the way of our health and well-being. Healthy ecosystems allow flexible exchange and sharing of resources between their inhabitants, thus helping each other to flourish.

Now, what elements of this course have helped you to turn your life into a more compassionate life, starting from the place where *you* are, day by day?

From formal to informal practice

So far, we have offered many formal practices that you could do in the time you especially set aside for them. There were also informal practices such as the Calendar Exercises, the Breathing Spaces and the Self-Compassion Mantra, which are not scheduled. These short practices can work like a bridge between the formal practice and the rest of your life, bringing kindness and compassion to your actual ecosystem, where it is needed most. In fact, there are numerous ways to bring the formal practice into your daily life. Here are just some examples.

– When you feel uncomfortable in situations from which you cannot escape, for instance in the chair at the dentist, you can imagine being in a safe place where you are accepted just the way you are.

- When you are stuck in a traffic jam, you can send kind wishes to drivers and passengers in cars around you.
- When an ambulance passes, you can send compassionate wishes to the people inside.
- When you face a difficult dilemma at work, you can take a Breathing Space and listen to your inner helper and to what a compassionate companion would advise you to do.
- When you wait at the bus stop, you can savour the warm sunrays on your face, or – more challenging if it rains – practise gratitude for the raindrops nourishing the earth.
- When your friend sends you the news of having passed her exam, you can take a moment to practise appreciative joy.
- When you helplessly witness an alcoholic colleague slipping back into bouts of heavy drinking, you can practise equanimity, realising you cannot take over somebody else's responsibilities.
- While you sit at the bedside of a sick relative or friend who is too weak to talk, you can practise Compassionate Breathing.
- When you feel powerless watching war and disaster on the news, you can send compassionate wishes to those who suffer from it.
- Finding yourself walking mechanically from A to B, you can decide to particularly notice what sensations fill you with joy or gratitude while you walk.
- And so on …

Be flexible, playful and creative in finding your own ways of transforming formal practices into informal ones. The short practices of the Breathing Spaces are particularly powerful in connecting formal and informal practice and switching from mindless doing to mindful being. In MBCT the Three-Minute Breathing Space is viewed as the cornerstone of the programme and offered with different emphases.[2] The first two phases are alike, but in the third phase various doors can be opened toward different fields requiring attention. Here is an adapted version of a Breathing Space for situations where action is required – after all, a lot of our daily life consists of decision-making and choosing actions. It can help to examine what motivates you and drives your actions – both in situations where you notice you operate on autopilot, and in situations where you face dilemmas and are in doubt as to what to do.

※ BREATHING SPACE FOR WISE COMPASSIONATE ACTION

1 Being present with open, kind awareness

As with the first phase of any Breathing Space, start with becoming aware of what your experience is right now, noticing physical sensations, thoughts and feelings just as they show up. Ask yourself 'What motivates me right now?' Do you perhaps sense

continued

the energy of the threat, drive or soothing systems? Do you notice any tendencies of moving toward or moving away, of seeking or avoiding experiences?

2 Allowing a soothing breathing rhythm

In the second phase, you can bring attention to the breath, gently allowing a soothing breathing rhythm to emerge, releasing tension you do not need to hold on to and feeling grounded.

3 Choosing wise compassionate action

In the third phase, while attuning to your body as a whole, you can ask yourself 'What would be wise and compassionate to choose, say or do right now?' Do you wish to choose from a threat, drive or caring motivation? What would be in line with your values? What would your inner helper or a compassionate companion advise you here? Proceed in the direction you wish to choose if this becomes clear enough. This may be the same direction as you went before, but now chosen mindfully and motivated with care. It may also be a different direction, one that seems kinder and more compassionate on closer examination. If you notice a lack of clarity as to how you wish to proceed, this is okay too. This can be an invitation to permit yourself more time and space to mindfully be with the situation before you do something. Just pause and relax with whatever shows itself, receiving it with a non-judgmental attitude of 'not-knowing'. Perhaps end with a wish that connects well, for instance 'May I be calm and patient', 'May I be with this dilemma until the right answer shows itself', or 'May my decisions be wise and caring, for myself and others'.

Action in deed

Some difficult situations require immediate action. In life-threatening sitations, you may well trust your survival instinct, otherwise it might be too late. In many other situations, you do not have to act immediately. When you are uncertain as to what is best, you may be better off taking a moment to *be* with the situation before you *do* something and take a Breathing Space as described above. Practising 'the sacred pause', as Tara Brach[3] refers to it, provides fertile ground for wise, compassionate action.

Pausing allows for mindful attuning to what the situation really needs, including yourself and the others involved, before you decide what to do. It may be wise not to act, giving yourself time to let the situation you face resonate in your heart and mind. Often, wisdom arises from an open attitude of 'not-knowing'. You can silently send a compassionate wish to yourself or others involved in the situation. You may also find the situation requires one of the other heart qualities right now, such as equanimity. Even if you feel helpless and powerless, you can 'do' something this way. You can practise relating wisely to this specific situation.

Or you may find you can indeed offer compassionate action. Examples are:

- Doing the shopping for a sick neighbour.
- Having a coffee with a new colleague.
- Sending a card to a bereaved friend.
- Taking the time to listen to someone sharing their difficulties, without needing to advise or offer quick solutions.
- Supporting or joining a charitable organisation.
- Doing something you are good at for someone who has difficulty with this, such as a DIY job, baking a cake or filling out a tax form.
- And don't forget to do something kind for yourself, such as treating yourself to something nourishing, soothing or energising. For instance, taking a hot bath, going for a walk, reading a favourite poem, visiting a friend or watching a film.

Practical ethics

Our greatest glory is not in never falling, but in rising every time we fall.
—Confucius

Talking about compassionate action, it may be good to say a few things about ethics. We do not mean the kind of ethics that tell us what is right or wrong and how we should behave, but in the sense of practical ethics. Of course, there are sensible rules that have stood the ages and are to be found in many traditions. Well known is the so-called Golden Rule, which says 'Treat others as you wish others to treat you'. Research consistently shows that altruism, generosity and prosocial behaviour not only benefit the ones who receive but also the ones who give.[4] The practice of mindfulness and compassion can increase our ethical consciousness as it gives us deeper insight into what heals and what harms. Seeing our lives in flux, interconnected with other beings in ever widening ecosystems, can make us aware that nothing that we do and say, or even think and imagine, is without consequences. If we do good, we serve the ecosystem, including ourselves. But just what 'good' means in a specific situation always needs careful assessment.

A helpful starting point for practical ethics is to mindfully acknowledge a situation in all its uniqueness and to compassionately sense what is needed. This is the kind of ethics you cannot learn by simply applying a set of rules. Only a non-judgmental, 'not-knowing' mind can assess the uniqueness of the situation you encounter. Ethical decisions need both heart and mind. Mindlessly following your heart has been called foolish compassion or 'mindless heart'.[5] For instance, pouring an alcoholic friend yet another drink. Meeting a situation with cold laser-beam attention without feeling into what the situation needs, could be called foolish mindfulness or 'heartless mind'. Wisdom – or heartful mind – is needed to discern what could have the most beneficial and the least harmful effects for as many beings involved as possible. It needs all the qualities of compassion – or mindful heart – to sense, resonate and feel into the needs of everyone involved. This kind of ethics can only come from a place of calmness, based in the soothing system. It is difficult to behave ethically when you are caught in threat or drive motivations, if you are fearful of making mistakes or craving for rewards.

If your life feels like a roller coaster, tossed around by threat and drive modes, steering yourself into calmer waters is not so easy at all. You may need the stabilising quality of equanimity and the following practice may be particularly helpful to explore. In the group training, we usually start session 7 with this formal practice of equanimity, which goes along similar lines to Kindness Meditation.

※ EQUANIMITY MEDITATION

Find yourself a comfortable position, beginning with the first two steps of the Breathing Space, mindfully acknowledging what is here right now … allowing soothing breathing and relaxation to enter the body… The words that have become known as the Serenity Prayer may give you a sense of equanimity: 'Grant me the serenity to accept the things I cannot change, the courage to change the things I can, and the wisdom to know the difference.' Also, metaphors may help you connect with the quality of equanimity, such as a stable solid mountain, a tranquil mirror-like lake or the attitude of the horse whisperer.

Then, bring somebody to mind who is more or less neutral to you, a passer-by whom you accidentally met in the street or in a queue lately … visualising this person in front of you, realising he or she is vulnerable to aging, disease, loss and death, like any human being … sending this person a wish of equanimity… For example, 'May you accept things as they are… May you feel calm and balanced amidst life's ups and downs… May you live in peace with impermanence and unpredictability…' You may turn to other neutral persons in the same way.

Then send a wish of equanimity towards yourself, e.g.

> *May I feel calm and balanced in the midst of life's turmoil… May I accept what comes and what goes… May I find harmony in joy and sadness, health and illness, success and failure… May I accept loss and be open to outcome… May I feel at ease with impermanence … with aging … with illness and death… May I accept I cannot change the past … have little control over the present … cannot predict the future … can only do what lies within my responsibility…*

If you feel very concerned about the behaviour of others, it may be helpful to realise that all individuals are ultimately responsible for their own actions. You could reflect or wish as follows: 'May I accept I cannot change others but I can offer them kindness and compassion…. May I discern wisely between what is within and what is outside my responsibility … between what is helpful and what is harmful.'

If you wish, you can expand the practice to one or more benefactors, good friends and dear persons. Also to difficult persons … it is not about accepting or condoning their behaviour, but about realising they are also vulnerable human beings, like you. A reflection with equanimity could be:

> *You are responsible for your own decisions and heir to the consequences of your own actions. I cannot make choices for you, but I can wish you discernment and wisdom... I cannot take away your suffering but I can wish you ease and peace...*

A wish in the we-form may also connect, e.g. 'May we find peace and harmony amidst life's difficulties.'

As with Kindness Meditation, you do not have to exclude any human, animal or other living creature from the practice of equanimity. You can also address groups. For people in areas of war and disaster, wishes could be: 'May you find calm amidst chaos ... ease amidst dis-ease ... inner peace amidst uncontrollability and unpredictability ... wisdom in a frantic world.'

You may conclude with:

> *May all beings feel calm amidst life's uncertainties... May all beings come to terms with impermanence, aging and dying... May all beings accept the comings and goings of life... May all beings find ease amidst harshness ... tranquility amidst turmoil ... balance amidst instability ... harmony amidst dissonance... May all beings live in peace with themselves and each other... May all beings know equanimity's peace of mind and spaciousness of heart... May there be peace for all.*

You may also wish to practise with another variation of the Kindness Meditation, where the quality of sympathetic joy is central to the wishes and reflections. This formal practice can be a particularly good remedy against unhealthy feelings of envy and jealousy.

※ SYMPATHETIC JOY MEDITATION

Find a comfortable position, mindfully pausing and allowing the breath to soothe your mind and body. First connect with a dear relative or friend whom you know enjoys good fortune or success in their actual life ... imagining this person in front of you, looking at the joy expressed by their body, face and eyes... Now imagine you feel the joy this person is feeling and send him or her a wish of sympathetic joy from your heart, e.g. 'May you celebrate this fortune... May you savour this success... May you enjoy happiness... May you appreciate the goodness of life...' Likewise, you can extend the practice to other dear persons in your life.

You can also treat yourself to similar wishes, thinking of something joyful that happened to you or that you experience right now, appreciating the feelings and sensations that come with it. Then let a celebrating wish flow towards yourself, e.g. 'May I appreciate this joy... May I celebrate the goodness in life... May I cherish this joy in my heart.'

You may then continue with other categories of persons. You may have come across someone of the neutral category, a passer-by you met and who from their body language,

continued

facial expression or tone of voice appeared to be joyful ... imagining this person in front of you and offering him or her wishes of sympathetic joy. 'May you appreciate and savour the joys of life'.

Now, the difficult person in this practice could be someone you tend to envy because of their fortunate circumstances or successes. The practice of sympathetic joy is a particularly good medicine when we experience strong feelings of envy or jealousy. Imagine someone you envy in front of you, realising this person wishes happiness, like you ... and allowing for an appreciative wish to flow to this person. 'May you enjoy your fortune... May you celebrate your successes... May you savour the goodness that life offers you... May you enjoy inner happiness ...' If you like, you can change to the we-form. 'May we celebrate the gifts of life... May our hearts fill with gratitude...' When this stirs up old bitterness, this can be acknowledged mindfully... You can always change to a compassionate wish towards yourself who experiences this bitterness right now, or return to appreciative wishes to a dear person.

Similarly, you can extend the practice to groups, if you feel the space to do so. Choose a group that recently shared in a joyful event or celebrated a success. You may belong to such a group yourself or know one from the news, for example a party that won the elections, or a sports club winning a match or a social media group that shared a joyful message. Letting congratulatory words and wishes flow to the group, like 'May you share and appreciate this joy... May you jointly celebrate this fortune... May you cherish this experience in your hearts...'

You may conclude with 'May all beings enjoy and share the goodness of life... May all beings be happy.'

Caring for the future

From caring comes courage.
—Lao Tzu

With only one session to go, we recommend that during the coming week you reflect on what can help sustain your practice and how to integrate what you have learned from the course into your daily life. What formal mindfulness and compassion practices could you keep up for a longer period and what informal practices would be good to regularly remind yourself of through the day? Give yourself plenty of opportunity to examine what motivates you moment by moment. Are you motivated by the threat, drive or soothing systems? Are your actions draining or sustaining your resources? Are you me-focussed, you-focussed or we-focussed? Are you serving the egosystem or the ecosystem? Are you true to what you really value? Do you choose your actions mindfully and heartfully?

Even if you do all you can to take good care of yourself and those around you, there may inevitably be periods of stress and risk of relapse into unfavourable ways. Especially at times when we are vulnerable, we can easily slip back into unhealthy habits and patterns. We therefore recommend that you look ahead, asking yourself how you might prevent and alleviate episodes of suffering in the future, particularly if you know you are prone to recurrence of stress-related problems, burnout, anxiety, depression or addiction. You may already have a relapse prevention plan. If this is so, you can look at it again and consider whether it needs any compassionate adjustments. If you do not have one, you may wish to make one.

※ A COMPASSIONATE PREVENTION PLAN

You can make use of the appropriate worksheet as a basic structure of the plan.
List the **stressful situations** *in your life that could provide a risk of relapse, for instance conflicts with others, the stress of deadlines at work, starting or ending relationships, feeling hurt, criticised or abandoned.*

Also list the **warning signals** *of imminent relapse. These could be concentration problems, persistent worries, mood changes, irritability, social withdrawal, sleeping problems, changes in your appetite, addictive behaviour, fatigue, headaches or other discomforts in the body. Be particularly aware of early warning signs. It is, for instance, important not to wait till your body screams with pain, but to notice and respond to the early whispers of discomfort.*

Then list the **compassionate do's and don'ts** *that can guide you when signs of relapse surface. How can you respond to early signs and also when the situation gets worse? What can you do to help yourself and what help could you ask for from others? What practices and previously proven remedies could help you? When and how would you seek professional help?*

In MBCT a distinction is made between activities that normally give you feelings of pleasure and those that give you a sense of mastery.[6] Both can be helpful to prevent your condition from getting worse. *Mastery activities* are not necessarily enjoyable, but they give you a feeling of having a grip on the situation. *Pleasure activities* may not be as enjoyable as when you are feeling good, but just doing them might still be better than putting them off. Sometimes, it can be wise to be firm with yourself and do more activities, for instance when you get stuck in unhealthy avoidance and stay in bed for too long. Sometimes, it can be wise to permit yourself to do fewer activities, particularly if you exhaust yourself in threat and drive modes. Depending on the situation, different strategies can be beneficial. The most important thing is that they come from a caring motivation.

Of course, you do not have to strive for perfection and finish your prevention plan in one go. You can work on it step by step. It is much more difficult to make a good plan when you are already in a wobbly phase. It is best to work on it in relatively stable periods. Feel free to adjust when you learn new things about yourself. Let it grow into a useful instrument that supports you when times get tough. Adding things to your plan like small symbolic objects, compassionate letters, comforting insights, inspiring quotes or poems, may turn it into a well-equipped 'Compassionate Survival Kit'.

※ Calendar: Giving Compassion

In the coming week you can explore situations in which you are aware of offering kindness or compassion to others, in heart, action or speech. You can take notes on what you observe in body, thoughts and feelings.

Questions for reflection

- What was the situation?
- How did you become aware of offering compassion?
- What physical sensations did you notice?
- What thoughts and emotions did you notice?
- What are you noticing now, while reflecting on this experience?

SUMMARY CHAPTER 7

In Chapter 7, the key themes are motivation and wise compassionate action in daily life, contemplating how we care for ourselves and others, distinguishing draining from sustaining activities and recognising what serves the ecosystem rather than the ego-system. We reflect on how to move on from formal to informal practice and how we can deepen the practice of equanimity and sympathic joy. The issue of practical ethics is raised and how we could prevent or alleviate recurrence of problems in the future.

SUGGESTIONS FOR PRACTICE

Formal

- Explore formal practices from previous chapters as required. If up to now you have done the Kindness Meditation or Compassionate Breathing with the help of audios, you can also try them without these and see whether it is possible to guide yourself. Or use the simpler Kindness Meditation – Whole Sequence 🔊.
- Alternate Kindness Meditation with the variations of Equanimity Meditation 🔊 or Sympathetic Joy Meditation 🔊.
- Work out A Day in Your Life 📝 and A Compassionate Prevention Plan 📝.

Informal

- Regularly practise the Breathing Spaces or Self-Compassion Mantra. Particularly pay attention to the Breathing Space for Wise Compassionate Action (p. 111) either when you have difficulty choosing what to do, or when you notice you are acting on autopilot.
- Calendar: Giving Compassion. 📝

Notes

1. Crocker, J. & Canevello, A. (2012). Egosystem and ecosystem: Motivational perspectives on caregiving. In S. L. Brown, R. M. Brown & L. A. Penner (eds), *Moving beyond self-Interest: Perspectives from evolutionary biology, neuroscience, and the social sciences* (pp. 211–223). New York: Oxford University Press.
2. Segal, S. V., Williams, J. M. G., & Teasdale, J. D. (2013). *Mindfulness-based cognitive therapy for depression.* New York: Guilford Press.
3. Brach, T. (2004). *Radical acceptance.* New York: Bantam.
4. Klein, S. (2014). *Survival of the nicest.* New York: The Experiment; Ricard, M. (2015). *Altruism.* London: Atlantic.
5. Gillis Chapman, S. (2012). *The five keys to mindful communication.* Boston & London: Shambala.
6. Segal, S. V., Williams, J. M. G., & Teasdale, J. D. (2013). *Mindfulness-based cognitive therapy for depression.* New York: Guilford Press.

Chapter 8

Healing life

Session eight: living with heart

From wonder into wonder existence opens.

—Lao Tzu

There is a story Jack Kornfield[1] tells about Thai monks who tended a large temple with an enormous clay statue of the Buddha. It was of plain appearance but very ancient and they cared for it respectfully. Although it had withstood the ages, the surface began to show so many cracks that they decided it needed to be repaired. A curious monk examined the statue more closely. He took out a flashlight and peered through one of the wider cracks. A brilliant golden flash shone back at him. He was thrilled and showed the other monks. With great care, they scraped off the clay and slowly a beautiful golden statue emerged. Apparently, monks who had lived in times of violence had decided to plaster it with clay to protect it from invaders, but nobody had survived to remember. Once it was uncovered, it became clear that this was one of the most precious golden Buddha images ever created in Southeast Asia. Nowadays, it attracts many devoted pilgrims from all over the country.

A crack in everything

Beneath pain, torment and brokenness, there may be richness and beauty waiting to be uncovered. There are many stories of people who grew stronger despite – or even thanks to – grave adversities. Some have become famous, such as Nelson Mandela and his struggle against apartheid. Twenty-seven years of harsh imprisonment did not prevent him becoming the first black president of South Africa. Or there is the story of Malala Yousafzai from Pakistan, who was shot because she stood up for her and other girls' rights to attend school. She survived her injuries, pursued her mission and became the youngest ever Nobel Peace Prize laureate.

There are countless lesser known stories about people discovering unexpected strengths during tough times. Working in health care, we encounter them daily. Everyone may be able to uncover their hidden gold inside by mindfully and heartfully attending to the cracks in their lives. As the late Leonard Cohen sang, it's the crack in everything that lets the light in. Life's imperfections may be our best teachers, opening our eyes to deeper values. A self-healing quality is present everywhere in nature, and if we can open our hearts to our wounds and losses, we may discover the power to heal ourselves from within, a shared experience that wisdom traditions have been referring to as our Innate Goodness.

Wounded healers

Some wounds cannot be healed, but even these can enable healing to take place at other levels. There is a Greek myth about the centaur Chiron who became known as the Wounded Healer.[2] Centaurs were half man, half horse and were often bold and fierce creatures. Chiron was a sensitive and wise centaur, however, who knew much about medicine and healing the sick. One day he was wounded by a poisoned arrow himself. Because of the strong poison the wound could not heal and he had to tend it daily with utmost care. He could not die from his wound and could not be freed from his suffering because he was immortal. The more skilful he became in nursing his wound, the better he got at helping others and he became a much-respected teacher in the art of healing. In the end, he was released from his own suffering when he willingly gave up his immortality.

If we learn to mindfully tend our wounds, sense what they need and take care of them in the best way we can, we learn skills that will benefit ourselves and others. In our modern societies, we tend to rely on professional healers who are trained to cure diseases and treat all kinds of problems for us. But they cannot cure the suffering that is an inevitable part of being human. We are responsible for this ourselves and the practice of mindfulness and compassion can be of great support here. It may not always bring freedom *from* suffering, but it can often bring freedom *within* suffering, right here, in the midst of our frantic world. There will always be imperfections we cannot cure, but we can become whole on a deeper level as we learn to live with them and give up our fixed or – referring to Chiron's story – 'immortalised' ideas about them. Thus, we can all become wounded healers.

We usually start the last session with an exercise the participants can choose, or an Appreciative Body Scan ◀)), or – if it has not already been offered in the silent session – the exercise below.

※ THE RIVER OF LIFE　　　　　　　　　　　　　　　　　27◀))

Find a comfortable position for a guided meditation, sitting or lying, kindly noticing whatever comes and goes. All experiences can be welcomed as part of the practice.

continued

Nothing specific needs to happen. Feel free to choose whether to follow the guidance or to follow your own path. Sometimes you might wish to dwell somewhere a bit longer, sometimes take less time. Both are fine. You do not have to work during the exercise, invite your imagination to work for you.

Imagine ... there is NOTHING... The first experience is yet to come. You don't even know what an experience is. There is nothing and you know nothing... And out of nothing the first experience arises, like a drop of water welling up from a spring. The first experience is the sensation of air flowing in through your nostrils ... the next drop is the sensation of air flowing out ... the sensations of the breath forming a tiny streamlet, held in the channel of your awareness, growing while more sensations of the breath emerge, in the nose, the throat, the chest, the belly ... becoming a rivulet, while the channel of your awareness adapts, effortlessly allowing the stream to flow ... expanding with other sensations from the body and the senses, arising out of nothing ... warmth and coolness, movement and rest, tension and relaxation, heaviness and lightness ... sensations of smell and taste, sounds and silence, near and far, light and dark, colour and shape... Sensations from inside and outside ... of touch and being touched ... pleasant and unpleasant ... the channel of awareness holding both without preference ... broadening effortlessly with the volume of the stream, holding a growing and flowing river, giving space to what comes and goes...

Besides awareness of what emerges inside and outside, there can be images and memories of times passed that show up in the stream of awareness, out of nothing... Memories from early childhood ... vivid or faint ... images of people you grew up with ... parents, grandparents, brothers or sisters, caregivers or mentors ... images of the surroundings you grew up in ... homes, friends, animals or toys you played with ... images from the past, now remembered, emerging out of nothing, painful or joyful ... the channel of your awareness widening without effort, giving space to what arises, letting go what dissolves ... Memories of kindergarten, schools, teachers, classmates ... things you learned, the hard way, the easy way... Memories of success and failure, reward and loss, ease and disease ... there is space in the channel of your awareness for everything, whether liked or disliked, cherished or despised... Yourself as a toddler, a primary school kid, a teenager, a student ... discovering an ever expanding world, discovering sexuality, delights and disappointments, making friends and losing touch, feeling loved and feeling unloved, ... moving and travelling, places where you lived, received schooling and worked, meeting people coming and going, harmonious and difficult relationships, feeling enriched and feeling lost... And if you notice rapids, waterfalls, obstructions, whirlpools ... allowing the channel of awareness to expand, allowing the stream to flow, becoming calmer and wider, offering space to whatever needs space... All images and memories of your history can join the stream, even the long-forgotten ones...

And for everything you ever identified with and identify with now, there is space in your awareness ... your qualities and skills, your talents and imperfections, tasks and roles, groups and networks ... for your beliefs and opinions, for all the stories you tell about yourself, others and the world ... for everything you connect 'I', 'me' or 'mine' with, there is space in the stream of awareness ... and also for everything you do not identify with, for every 'not-I', 'not-me', 'not-mine' there is space ... for 'us' and for 'them', for friend and foe... Everything that feels close and everything that feels remote can join the stream...

Not only past and present, also images of the time ahead can be held in the channel of awareness ... plans and dreams, promises the future holds, hopes and fears, subtle intuitions and heartfelt wishes, visions of harmony and peace as well as doom and gloom, images of heaven and hell ... for all intentions and commitments there is space, also for what is yet unknown, even for the unimaginable...

And so, allowing the river to grow and held by an ever widening and deepening channel of awareness, effortlessly adjusting to whatever needs space ... the banks of the river moving so far apart that from one side you cannot see the other ... ever vaster, ever deeper ... the river becoming a sea ... and the sea becoming an ocean ... boundlessly wide, boundlessly deep ... a heart as big as the world ... offering space for EVERYTHING...

The river of life flows between the wisdom of nothing and the love of everything.[3]

At home wherever you go

One of the first exercises we introduced in this book was to imagine being in a safe place, where you are accepted just the way you are. This last exercise offers a metaphor for how your heart and mind can offer a safe place to all your experience just the way it is, with openness and equanimity. You can explore how this metaphor works for you by revisiting it on different occasions.

Can you both relate intimately to the tiniest drop of experience and open widely towards the boundless ocean of possibilities? It may seem quite impossible if you see it as something to strive for, but it may well be your natural state, once you stop striving being someone other than you are becoming moment by moment. When you allow your life to unfold like a flowing river. Without the push of getting away (threat system) or the pull of getting ahead (drive system), but with the ease of getting along (soothing system) with your experiences as they come and go, you may feel at home wherever you go.

In the last session we harvest what the participants share about the course and contemplate together how they can continue their journeys on the path of mindful compassion.

We invite you to reflect on the following questions.

Questions for reflection

- What did you expect when you embarked on this course or began to work through this book? You can look back at what you wrote down on Worksheet 1 – Desired Outcome.
- What did you learn on the way?
- What was difficult and what was helpful?
- What do you wish to continue? Which formal and informal practices? What could offer support?
- Is there a symbol, a little object, card, poem or quote that expresses what the course stands for and can work as a helpful reminder in the future?

Like many participants in the course, you may have learned things you did not expect. You may have found something valuable in the difficult. Perhaps some of your desired consequences have been fulfilled, while others have not. There may be a lot of work in progress. Although the course is coming to an end, the journey will continue. It is the same at the end of a mindfulness course, when we say that the last session of the course does not end here. It extends into the rest of your life.

Tending your inner garden

To help you make choices for ongoing practice, you may wish to look at the session overview on pp. 154–155, which you can also download. We can divide the practices in this course into three categories, using the metaphor of how you would tend a garden. In fact, practising mindful compassion is very much like doing inner gardening. It is like cultivating the 'good', coping with the 'bad' and caring for the 'ugly'[4] – of course, not to be taken in any moral sense.

Cultivating the good – growing the flowers of mindfulness and heartfulness

Just as you can choose to grow fruits, vegetables or flowers in a garden outdoors you can decide to grow mindfulness and wholesome qualities in your inner garden. In an outdoor garden, you need the right conditions for your plants to thrive such as the right climate, light, humidity and nourishment. However, you also need to care for the plants, giving them attention, water and fertiliser, trimming and providing them with supports, picking what is ripe and composting what is withering. Likewise, you need good conditions for your inner qualities to grow. It involves setting and resetting your intentions, committing yourself to your values and taking time to practise, formally and informally, on a regular basis. This category includes informal practices like the Soothing Breathing Rhythm, the Breathing Space with Kindness and nourishing the soothing system through the senses, for instance by going for a Pleasure Walk. Formal practices in this category are the imagery practices A Safe Place, A Compassionate Companion and Embodying Compassion. Other formal practices are the ones derived from traditions nourishing the Four Friends for Life: Kindness Meditation, Compassionate Breathing, Equanimity Meditation and Sympathetic Joy Meditation. Furthermore, there are Kindness to the Body, an Appreciative Body Scan, Walking and Moving with Kindness, Revisiting the Good and the practice of Gratitude. And remember the many opportunities to allow formal practices to informally infuse your daily activities.

Coping with the bad – wisely addressing difficulties as they arise

Just as weeds, pests, heat or frost, drought or floods can harm your garden plants, difficulties can arise in daily life that could harm your inner garden. There are various practices that may help you cope with harmful conditions. For example, some informal practices for when you are facing stress or dilemmas are the Breathing Spaces of the coping variety – with Compassion, Compassionate Breathing and for Wise Compassionate Action. The Self-Compassion Mantra is another useful exercise for an emergency and there are formal practices that help explore and compassionately deal with the automatic reactivity we get easily caught in, such as Compassionately Relating to Resistance, Desire or Inner Patterns, or addressing a Compassionate Letter to yourself in this difficult situation. You may not need to do these on a regular basis but as required, just as you do not need to weed or water your garden every day if the conditions are good.

Caring for the ugly – special care for unhealed wounds

Some garden plots may be so infertile, wasted or polluted that nothing grows there. They need special care and a skilled gardener to re-fertilise the poor soil. Likewise, there may be seriously hurt, rejected or hardened parts in yourself that need special care. These inner deserts may have serious difficulty receiving kindness and react with backdraft. They require greater sensitivity, patience and loving kindness in manageable portions. It needs fine-tuning to choose the practices that connect best here, carefully listening to these suffering parts and their deeper needs. Suitable practices may be: imagining that your suffering is held within a safe place, by a compassionate companion or by yourself embodying compassion. Other possibilities include gentle compassionate breathing, compassionate letter writing, kindness practice with difficult persons or forgiveness practice. In addition, working with metaphors like the horse whisperer or the flowing river, can be supportive here.

However, gardeners know it is important not to water certain plants too carefully. If they make life too easy for them, the roots don't go looking for water and so they stay small and weak. It is the less perfect conditions that encourage plants to grow strong and become resilient. So, dealing with the bad and the ugly may actually be the most powerful ways to cultivate the good. When we learn to deal with setbacks we become more resilient and grow in strength. Resilience has been embraced as a new definition of health for people and communities.[5] Health is neither the absence of disease, nor a state of well-being in ideal circumstances. It is the capacity to grow and thrive in imperfect conditions.

Further support

So, there are many ways to tend your inner garden. Some do daily formal practice, others now and then. Some find it hard to practise informally if they do not keep up their formal practice, while others find this comes quite naturally. Some are happy practising on their own, while others need the support of smaller or larger meditation groups, on a regular basis or on occasional retreats. In many places, there are guided meditation groups to find in various traditions or as booster sessions at mindfulness centres. Other possibilities are online facilities and self-support groups, where participants practise in silence, use audio material or guide each other in turns. We regularly see groups like this being spontaneously formed at the end of training courses. Mindful communication courses are also increasingly being offered and can deepen your practice.

You can check out books for further reading at the end of this chapter. Do not hesitate to seek professional help from a teacher, counsellor or therapist if you meet with difficulties that feel too much to be working with alone. Do not consider this as a failure but as an act of kindness to yourself.

If you have used this book as a self-help guide you may still consider joining an MBCL training course, as many participants have said how much they appreciate sharing this path in the common humanity experience of a group. Teachers are increasingly being trained and a register of certified trainers can be found at www.compassionateliving.info.

Spreading your wings

> *For the bird of enlightenment to fly, it must have two wings: the wing of wisdom and the wing of compassion.*
>
> —Zen saying

We do not consider enlightenment to be an ultimate state to arrive at as a reward for strenuous practice. We find it more helpful to view it as a process open to all in everyday situations, when we wake up – 'enlighten' – to what shows itself and let our hearts resonate with it. Wisdom and compassion need to be awakened again and again in the unique situations we encounter. You can only discover what this means by travelling your own path. No one has ever walked this path before. So, take your steps with care, mindfully and heartfully. Then, the hidden gold inside you can reveal itself step by step.

> *May you be safe.*
> *May you be free from suffering and find wholeness in the imperfections of life.*
> *May you enjoy inner happiness and live in peace with yourself and those around you.*
> *May you spread your wings of wisdom and compassion and bring healing to yourself and those whose lives you touch.*

SUMMARY CHAPTER 8

In Chapter 8 we reflect on how mindful compassion can facilitate our self-healing capacity and how we can become wounded healers. Another metaphor is offered in the River of Life 🔊. We have offered many practices that can help to cultivate the good that you may do on a regular basis, formally and informally; others you may do when there is a need to help you deal wisely with difficulties as they arise and are faced with wounded parts needing special care.

SUGGESTIONS FOR PRACTICE

- You can evaluate the course reflecting on the questions of the worksheet. 📝
- We invite you to offer yourself suggestions which practices you will do in the weeks to come.
- A concise summary of the whole course is offered in the session overview on pp. 154–155 📝 to remind you of key themes and practices in the future.

Notes

1   Kornfield, J. (2009). *The wise heart* (pp. 11–12). New York: Bantam.
2   https://en.wikipedia.org/wiki/Chiron, accessed 3 July 2017.
3   Inspired by Sri Nisargadatta, as quoted in: Sudhakar S. Dikshit (ed.) (2012). *I am that: Talks with Sri Nisargadatta Maharaj*. Durham, NC: The Acorn Press.
4   With a playful nod to Sergio Leone's film *The Good, the Bad and the Ugly* (1966).
5   Zautra, A. J., Hall, J. S., & Murray, K. E. (2010). Resilience: A new definition of health for people and communities. In J. R. Reich, A. J. Zautra, & J. S. Hall (eds). *Handbook of adult resilience* (pp. 3–30). New York: Guilford.

Audio downloads

The following mp3 files can be downloaded from www.routledge.com/9781138228931 for personal, non-commercial use.

1 Breathing Space with Kindness
2 A Safe Place
3 Kindness Meditation: Yourself
4 Compassionately Relating to Resistance
5 Breathing Space with Compassion
6 A Compassionate Companion
7 Kindness Meditation: A Benefactor
8 Compassionately Relating to Desire
9 Compassionately Relating to Inner Patterns
10 Kindness Meditation: A Good Friend
11 Embodying Compassion
12 Kindness Meditation: A Neutral Person
13 Kindness for the Body
14 Walking with Kindness
15 Kindness Meditation: A 'Difficult' Person
16 Compassionate Breathing: Yourself
17 Compassionate Breathing: Others
18 Revisiting the Good
19 Forgiving Yourself
20 Asking Forgiveness
21 Forgiving Others
22 Kindness Meditation: Groups and All Beings
23 An Appreciative Body Scan
24 The Horse Whisperer
25 Equanimity Meditation
26 Sympathetic Joy Meditation
27 The River of Life
28 Kindness Meditation: Whole Sequence

Worksheet downloads

The following pdf files can be downloaded from www.routledge.com/9781138228931 for personal, non-commercial use.

1 Desired Outcome
2 General Progress
3 A Safe Place
4 Kindness to Yourself
5 Calendar: Soothing System
6 Compassionately Relating to Resistance
7 A Compassionate Companion
8 Calendar: Threat System
9 Compassionately Relating to Desire
10 Recognising Inner Patterns
11 Compassionately Relating to Inner Patterns
12 Calendar: Drive System
13 Doing as If
14 Embodying Compassion
15 Calendar: Inner Critic
16 Calendar: Inner Helper
17 Forgiving Yourself
18 Gratitude
19 Your Values
20 Calendar: Receiving Compassion
21 A Day in Your Life
22 Compassionate Prevention Plan
23 Calendar: Giving Compassion
24 Evaluation of the Course
25 Session Overview

1   Desired Outcome

What do you wish to come out of this training, regarding...
- how you relate to yourself?
- how you relate to others (family, friends, colleagues, etc.)?
- how you deal with current difficulties in your life?
- how you engage with other areas in your life that are important to you (e.g. education and work, health and lifestyle, social activities, nature and spirituality)?
- how you work towards valuable goals in your life, short term and long term?
- how you deal with future challenges?

2   General Progress

Week ...	Observations, insights, challenges, questions?

Day 1
 	
What exercises did you practise?
 	
Practice time?
  -   formal   ... minutes
  - informal ... minutes	

Day 2
 	
What exercises did you practise?
 	
Practice time?
  -   formal   ... minutes
  - informal ... minutes	

Day 3
 	
What exercises did you practise?
 	
Practice time?
  -   formal   ... minutes
  - informal ... minutes	

Day 4
 	
What exercises did you practise?
 	
Practice time?
  -   formal   ... minutes
  - informal ... minutes	

Day 5
 	
What exercises did you practise?
 	
Practice time?
  -   formal   ... minutes
  - informal ... minutes	

Day 6
 	
What exercises did you practise?
 	
Practice time?
  -   formal   ... minutes
  - informal ... minutes	

3   A Safe Place

Which place(s) arose during the exercise?	Which senses were you most aware of during the exercise?	Which bodily sensations, feelings and thoughts did you observe?	What was it like to imagine that the place really appreciated you were there?	What are you noticing now, while reflecting on the exercise? What could be a kind wish to yourself?
Example: *First there were no clear images but then an experience at the seaside came up.*	*There was a felt sense of lying on a warm sandy beach. I heard sounds of breaking waves and seagulls. I smelled the sea.*	*I began to feel more comfortable and at ease. A long-forgotten childhood memory came up.*	*At first it got me into thinking how this could be possible. Then it was as if the place really cared about me. It touched my heart.*	*The same warm feelings arise now. I feel touched again, both joy and tears come up. 'May I feel accepted just the way I am.'*
Day 1				
Day 2				
Day 3				
Day 4				
Day 5				
Day 6				

4   Kindness to Yourself

	What wish(es) connected most with you?	Which physical sensations did you notice while you practised?	Which thoughts and feelings did you observe?	What was noticeable in the giving and the receiving of the wish(es)?	What are you noticing now, while reflecting on the practice? What could be a kind wish now?
Day 1					
Day 2					
Day 3					
Day 4					
Day 5					
Day 6					

5   Calendar: Soothing System

What was the situation?	How and when did you become aware of the soothing system?	Which bodily experiences did you notice?	Which thoughts and feelings did you notice?	What are you noticing right now? What could be a kind wish to yourself?
Example: *It was lovely weather. I had lunch in the park, sitting on my favourite bench, mindfully eating my sandwich, watching the ducks in the pond.*	*I noticed my awareness opening to the surroundings and my breathing becoming deeper.*	*My body felt relaxed. I felt softness in my face and my belly. I noticed the tasty food and the warm sunrays on my face.*	*I thought 'This is a nice way to have lunch!' I felt happy and grateful.*	*It makes me feel warm and thankful again. 'May I take good care of myself.'*
Day 1				
Day 2				
Day 3				
Day 4				
Day 5				
Day 6				

6 Compassionately Relating to Resistance

What situation did you choose?

What did you notice whilst embodying 'No'?

How would it be to persist with 'No' in this situation?

What did you notice whilst embodying 'Yes' or 'Okay'?

How would it be to persist with 'Yes' in this situation?

Are there aspects to this situation where 'No' would be more fitting or 'Yes' would be more fitting? (For instance, saying 'No' to offensive behaviour from another person, whilst saying 'Yes' to your feelings.)

What could be a kind wish to yourself or others regarding the theme you have explored?

7 A Compassionate Companion

What being(s) appeared during the exercise?	Which sense qualities were most clearly present (seeing, hearing, smelling, feeling)?	Which physical sensations, thoughts and feelings did you notice?	What was it like to imagine the compassionate being really appreciated you?	What are you noticing now, while reflecting on the exercise? What could be a kind wish now?
Example: *First there was nothing much. Then a surprising image appeared of a horse that looked at me kindly.*	*The visual sense was clearest, especially the love and wisdom speaking from the eyes. Later I also smelled its presence and felt its strong body.*	*I felt warmth and joy in my chest. Later I felt very peaceful, my thoughts drifted off to my childhood. For a moment I fell asleep.*	*It was as if all sensations became more intense. It brought tears to my eyes.*	*I am touched by the exercise. The image comes alive again. 'May I allow myself to be touched by kindness.'*
Day 1				
Day 2				
Day 3				
Day 4				
Day 5				
Day 6				

8   Calendar: Threat System

What was the situation?	How and when did you become aware of the threat system?	Which physical sensations did you notice?	Which thoughts and emotions did you notice?	What are you noticing now, while reflecting on this experience? What could be a compassionate response?
Example: *My manager sent me an email with the request to see him before the end of the day. I immediately tensed up.*	*I first felt very uncomfortable and a sense of doom came over me. Then I realised: this is my alarm bell going off.*	*My muscles tightened (jaws, shoulders). My breath became shallow. I felt my heartbeat.*	*I had a frightening thought: 'Now it's my turn. I will be made redundant.' I felt anxious and worried all day.*	*I notice relief and a smile. All he asked me was to take on a new project. Next time when I imagine disaster I will take a breathing space with compassion.*
Day 1				
Day 2				
Day 3				
Day 4				
Day 5				
Day 6				

9   Compassionately Relating to Desire

What area of desire or attachment did you explore?
Which physical sensations, thoughts and feelings did you notice?
What answer(s) came up with the question: 'Is there anything that lies underneath this desire?'
What did you wish for yourself? How was this received inside?
What is happening now, while you reflect on the exercise? What could be a kind or compassionate wish right now?

10   Recognising Inner Patterns

Look at the list of 19 sentences below and read through them one by one. Pause after each sentence and give a score in the column Recognisability: 1 = this I don't recognise at all in my life; 2 = this I recognise somewhat; 3 = this I fairly recognise; 4 = this I recognise well; 5 = this I strongly recognise.

In giving a score, follow your first inclination and pay more attention to the sphere of the sentences than the precise words. Score from what the sentence 'feels' like, instead of giving it a lot of thought.

Inner pattern	Recognisability
1. My close relationships will end because people are unreliable and unpredictable.	1 2 3 4 5
2. I expect that others will hurt me and take advantage of me.	1 2 3 4 5
3. I can't seem to get what I need from others (warmth, attention, understanding, protection, support).	1 2 3 4 5
4. I'm defective, bad, not okay, and don't deserve to be loved by others.	1 2 3 4 5
5. I'm alone in this world, different from others, I do not belong.	1 2 3 4 5
6. I'm boring and totally uninteresting to other people; they don't want me in their company.	1 2 3 4 5
7. I'm not capable of living my life; I need help to take care of myself and to make decisions.	1 2 3 4 5
8. A disaster might happen any moment, and I won't be able to cope.	1 2 3 4 5
9. I feel empty, confused, lost without guidance from my elders.	1 2 3 4 5
10. I'm a failure, I'm stupid, inept, and will never be successful compared to others.	1 2 3 4 5
11. I deserve whatever I can get; others need to take my wishes into account.	1 2 3 4 5
12. I'm easily frustrated, react impulsively or throw in the towel.	1 2 3 4 5
13. I adapt to what others want from me, out of fear for their anger or rejection.	1 2 3 4 5
14. I suppress my own needs and emotions in order to be of service to others.	1 2 3 4 5
15. For me, everything revolves around getting recognition and appreciation from others.	1 2 3 4 5
16. I presume that whatever can go wrong will go wrong, and that my decisions will not work out.	1 2 3 4 5
17. I prefer not to show my feelings (positive or negative) to others and would rather take a more rational approach.	1 2 3 4 5
18. I'm a perfectionist, need to spend my time efficiently, and abide strictly by the rules.	1 2 3 4 5
19. I'm impatient with others and with myself, and insist that people should be punished for their mistakes.	1 2 3 4 5

11   Compassionately Relating to Inner Patterns

Regarding the pattern you have chosen to explore...
How and when did this pattern arise in your life? Are there any particular experiences at the root of this pattern?
How did the pattern develop itself further? What experiences strengthened the pattern in the course of your life?
Did and does the pattern have unintended consequences and contribute to your own or others' suffering? If yes, in what ways?
What about the activity of the emotion regulation systems (threat, drive or soothing) in this pattern? What about a particular stress reaction (fight, flight, freeze or tend and befriend)?
Did you develop this pattern on purpose? To what extent was it an attempt to survive or deal with difficult circumstances?
Has the pattern helped you or has it been beneficial in any way? Is this still so? If yes, how?
Could you give the pattern a playful name? Let it be a name that brings a smile on your face, opens your heart and softens your relationship with the pattern. What could be a compassionate wish to yourself related to this pattern?

12   Calendar: Drive System

What was the situation?	How and when did you become aware of the drive system?	Which physical sensations did you notice?	Which thoughts and emotions did you notice?	What are you noticing now, while reflecting on this experience? What could be a compassionate response?
Example: *During meditation, I did my very best to connect with the compassionate companion I had the day before.*	*It took a while before I noticed I was working so hard. Then I noticed feeling hot and my body leaning forward.*	*My forehead and eyes felt tight. There was tension in my chest and shoulders.*	*I thought: 'I want this good feeling back I had yesterday. I must try harder.' I felt frustrated that I could not do it.*	*I notice myself smiling. While I write this down, an image of a laid back compassionate companion surprises me. 'May I be patient with myself.'*
Day 1				
Day 2				
Day 3				
Day 4				
Day 5				
Day 6				

13   Doing as If

Describe your experiences of experiment 1 – Doing as If you feel angry.

Describe your experiences of experiment 2 – Doing as If you feel joyful.

What did you learn from these two experiments? What do you take with you?

14 Embodying Compassion

While imagining yourself as a compassionate being, what sensations did you notice in the body?	What did you notice in your thoughts and feelings?	How did embodying compassion affect the inner attitude towards yourself, others and the world around you?	What are you noticing now, while you reflect on the experience of the exercise?	When you imagine yourself embodying compassion, what could be a compassionate response to a current difficulty in your life?
Example: *My muscles softened. My body felt grounded, calm, open and dignified.*	*Some doubt crept in: 'I am making this up. This can't be real.' When I noted these thoughts as thoughts, they cleared. I felt confident and brave.*	*I felt both connected with myself and with others. It was a new feeling.*	*I feel surprised, moved and grateful for being able to experience this.*	*I don't have to give in to others when we plan holidays at work. If I take care of myself I can care for others better.*
Day 1				
Day 2				
Day 3				
Day 4				
Day 5				
Day 6				

15 Calendar: Inner Critic

What was the situation?	How did you become aware of the inner critic?	What did the inner critic say to you?	What did you notice in your body and emotions?	What are you noticing now, while reflecting on this experience? What could be a compassionate response?
My manager praised me for a little job I did. After she left my inner critic started up.	I felt a dark, heavy feeling coming over me as soon as it sank in what she said.	'You know you don't deserve this. She will soon get back with a list of all the things you did wrong.'	I tensed up, my breath became shallow and I felt my stomach squeeze. I felt anxious and mistrustful.	I now feel she really meant it, she was kind to me all day. Well done, I recognised my inner critic! 'May I be open to compliments.'
Day 1				
Day 2				
Day 3				
Day 4				
Day 5				
Day 6				

16   Calendar: Inner Helper

What was the situation?	How did you become aware of the inner helper?	What did the inner helper say to you?	What did you notice in your body and emotions?	What do you notice now while you reflect on this experience? What could be a kind response?
I corrected myself kindly after having made a mistake at work.	I noticed a first impulse to get angry with myself but then I noticed I needed something else.	'We all make mistakes at times. You were very tired and it is understandable. You can simply correct it.'	I felt my body ease and noticed a smile coming up. I felt warmth in my chest.	While I would have criticised myself harshly in the past, I now feel how beneficial it is to offer myself understanding. 'May I trust my inner wisdom.'
Day 1				
Day 2				
Day 3				
Day 4				
Day 5				
Day 6				

17   Forgiving Yourself

Which area of inner harshness did you explore?

What did you notice in your body, emotions and thoughts?

How did this area of inner harshness develop?

Did you do it on purpose? Could you foresee the consequences at the time?

What was it like to offer yourself forgiveness? Was there a word, wish, image or gesture that had a softening effect?

What are you noticing now, while reflecting on this exercise? What could be a kind wish for yourself right now?

18   Gratitude

What fills you with gratitude? (circumstances, others, personal qualities)

What is it exactly that strikes the gratitude chord in you? How is this experienced in your body, feelings and thoughts?

What are you noticing now while reflecting on this?

19 Your Values

1. What are your values, what do you wish your life to stand for?

2. How do you give expression to these values in your daily life?

3. What stands in the way of expressing your values?

4. What could support you in expressing your values? What could be a kind wish to yourself?

20   Calendar: Receiving Compassion

What was the situation?	How did you become aware of receiving compassion?	Which physical sensations did you notice?	Which thoughts and emotions did you notice?	What do you notice now, while reflecting on this experience?
I paid a first visit to a friend who just moved, but I got lost and felt anxious in a town I did not know. A passer-by offered me help.	*At first I was on my guard, but then his kind face and sympathetic voice made me feel he really wished to help me.*	*At first I felt a little tense but then I relaxed and smiled back at him.*	*I felt relief and gratitude. I thought: 'What a nice chap. Thanks to him I can still arrive on time.'*	*When I think back of his kind face and lovely smile my heart fills with joy.*
Day 1				
Day 2				
Day 3				
Day 4				
Day 5				
Day 6				

21   A Day in Your Life

Daily activities	Care for yourself (1–5)	Care for others (1–5)

22   Compassionate Prevention Plan

Risk situations

Warning signals

Helpful (compassionate do's)

Not helpful (compassionate don'ts)

23   Calendar: Giving Compassion

What was the situation?	How did you become aware of offering compassion?	Which physical sensations did you notice?	Which thoughts and emotions did you notice?	What are you noticing now, while reflecting on this experience?
My neighbour caught me at the door when I was in a hurry. She said she was made redundant at work. When I saw tears in her eyes I decided to make time for her.	I allowed a soothing breathing rhythm and imagined embodying compassion while I listened to her, silently sending her kind wishes.	The tension in my body softened and my heart melted when I turned towards her.	A first thought 'Not now', soon changed into 'I wish I could ease your pain'. I felt her distress but felt also courage to be with her.	I feel connected with her. I am glad I could give her some time and feel touched by her embrace when she thanked me for listening.
Day 1				
Day 2				
Day 3				
Day 4				
Day 5				
Day 6				

24 Evaluation of the Course

| **What did you expect when you embarked on this course or began to work through this book?** |
| You can look back at what you wrote down on Worksheet 1 Desired Outcome. |
| |

| **What did you learn on the way? What was difficult and what was helpful?** |
| |

| **What do you wish to continue? Which formal and informal practices? What could offer support?** |
| |

| **Is there a symbol, a little object, card, poem or quote that expresses what the course stands for and can work as a helpful reminder in the future?** |
| |

25   Session Overview

SESSION	1 How we evolved – Threat, drive and soothing systems	2 Threat and self- compassion	3 Untangling desires and patterns	4 Embodying compassion
THEMES	Why (not) practise compassion? Multi-layered brain *The design is not our fault* The three systems and their balance How to nourish the soothing system?	Reactions to outer and inner threat: *Fight, flight, freeze, tend and befriend* and their disguises Pathways to self-compassion Backdraft and other obstacles	Desire and satisfaction Healthy and unhealthy patterns Inner critic and self-conscious emotions (shame, shyness, guilt, envy)	Flow directions of compassion The Lotus of Compassion: atmosphere, attributes, skills Feeding an inner helper
PRACTICES • AS REQUIRED	Contemplating the Three Systems in Your Life	Compassionately Dealing with Resistance	Compassionately Dealing with - Desire - Inner Patterns	
• REGULAR IMAGERY KINDNESS MEDITATION OTHER	 A Safe Place Self Pleasure Walk	 A Compassionate Companion Benefactor ...*continue*...	 ...*continue*... Dear Person ...*continue*...	 Embodying Compassion Neutral Person Kindness for Body Moving/ Walking with Kindness
• INFORMAL CALENDAR	Breathing Space (BS) with Kindness Soothing system	BS with Compassion Self-Compassion Mantra Threat system	...*continue*... Drive system	...*continue*... Inner critic

5 Self and others – Widening the circle	6 Growing happiness	SILENT PRACTICE SESSION: e.g. Kindness Meditation–Imagery–Walking–Moving–Appreciative Body Scan–Metaphors (see 8)	7 Weaving wisdom and compassion into daily life	8 Living with Heart
Who are *you* The problem with over-identifying Kindness to others and its challenges A wordless alternative	Three doors to happiness: Pleasant life Engaged life Meaningful life Four Friends for Life: Kindness Compassion Sympathetic Joy Equanimity		Motivated by threat, drive or care? Draining or sustaining, ego- or ecosystem From formal to informal practice Practical ethics	Healing power of compassion Evaluation How to continue? Tending your inner garden
Compassionate Letter Writing	Forgiving Yourself Asking Forgiveness Forgiving Others		A Day in Your Life Prevention Plan	Metaphors: - River of Life - Horse Whisperer
Compassionate Breathing Self/Others 'Difficult' Person *…continue…*	Revisiting the Good Groups All Beings Gratitude Silver Lining Values		*…continue…* Focus on Equanimity or Sympathetic Joy *…continue…*	*…continue…* *…continue…* *…continue…*
BS with Compassionate Breathing Inner helper	*…continue…* Receiving compassion		BS for Wise Compassionate Action Giving compassion	*…continue…*

Further reading

Here are just a few titles out of the rapidly expanding literature, suitable for a wide audience.

Karen Armstrong, *Twelve steps to a compassionate life*. The Bodley Head, 2011.

James Baraz & Shoshana Alexander, *Awakening joy*. Bantam, 2010.

Tara Brach, *Radical acceptance*. Bantam, 2004.

Brené Brown, *Daring greatly*. New York City, NY: Gotham, 2012.

Vidyamala Burch & Danny Penman, *Mindfulness for health*. Piatkus, 2013.

Pema Chödrön, *Tonglen*. Vajradhatu Publications, 2001.

HH the Dalai Lama & Archbishop Desmond Tutu, with Douglas Abrams: *The book of joy*. Penguin, 2016.

Christina Feldman, *Boundless heart*. Shambhala, 2017.

Barbara Fredrickson, *Love 2.0*, Penguin Putnam Inc, 2013.

Christopher Germer, *The mindful path to self-compassion*. Guilford Press, 2009.

Paul Gilbert & Choden, *Mindful compassion*. New Harbinger Publications, 2013.

Susan Gillis Chapman, *The Five Keys To Mindful Communication*. Shambhala 2012.

Rick Hanson, *Hardwiring happiness*. Ebury Press, 2013.

Chris Irons & Elaine Beaumont, *The compassionate mind workbook*. Constable and Robinson, 2017.

Thupten Jinpa, *A fearless heart*. Avery, 2015.

Kristin Neff, *Self-compassion.* Hodder & Stoughton, 2011.

Matthieu Ricard, *Altruism.* Atlantic, 2015.

Sharon Salzberg, *Loving-kindness.* Shambala, 1995.

Daniel Siegel, *Mindsight.* Bantam, 2010.

Mark Williams & Danny Penman, *Mindfulness: A practical guide to finding peace in a frantic world.* Piatkus, 2011.

Index